中国科学院大学
研究生教材系列

学科英语写作教程
地学

Writing a
Research Paper in
Geoscience

总主编◎高　原　张红晖
主　编◎刘云龙

清华大学出版社
北京

内容简介

本书共七章，系统讲解学术英语论文中标题、摘要、引言、方法、结果、讨论、总结与致谢的写作规范；每章包含整体概述、案例分析、功能句型、时态分析、重要语法点等具体内容，配有题型丰富、形式新颖、针对性强的练习，旨在帮助地学相关专业的学生系统了解并掌握本领域重点期刊英文论文的写作规范、结构、语步、常用词汇、功能句型等内容，全面提升其学术论文写作水平与学术思辨能力。所设练习均以真实性为首要原则，充分考虑学生可能遇到的学术阅读与写作场景。

本书适合国内高校地学相关专业的高年级本科生与硕博研究生使用，也可供地学科研工作者参考。

版权所有，侵权必究。举报：010-62782989，beiqinquan@tup.tsinghua.edu.cn。

图书在版编目（CIP）数据

学科英语写作教程：地学 / 高原，张红晖总主编；刘云龙主编 . —北京：清华大学出版社，2022.11

中国科学院大学研究生教材系列

ISBN 978-7-302-62131-7

Ⅰ．①学… Ⅱ．①高… ②张… ③刘… Ⅲ．①地球科学—英语—写作—研究生—教材 Ⅳ．① H319.36

中国版本图书馆 CIP 数据核字（2022）第 204672 号

责任编辑：方燕贝
封面设计：李尘工作室
责任校对：王凤芝
责任印制：丛怀宇

出版发行：清华大学出版社
网　　址：http://www.tup.com.cn, http://www.wqbook.com
地　　址：北京清华大学学研大厦A座　　邮　编：100084
社 总 机：010-83470000　　邮　购：010-62786544
投稿与读者服务：010-62776969, c-service@tup.tsinghua.edu.cn
质量反馈：010-62772015, zhiliang@tup.tsinghua.edu.cn

印 装 者：三河市君旺印务有限公司
经　　销：全国新华书店
开　　本：185mm×260mm　　印　张：10.25　　字　数：226千字
版　　次：2022年12月第1版　　印　次：2022年12月第1次印刷
定　　价：56.00元

产品编号：091874-01

总　　序

2020 年 11 月，教育部新文科建设工作组发布的《新文科建设宣言》指出："文科教育融合发展需要新文科。新科技和产业革命浪潮奔腾而至，社会问题日益综合化复杂化，应对新变化、解决复杂问题亟需跨学科专业的知识整合，推动融合发展是新文科建设的必然选择。进一步打破学科专业壁垒，推动文科专业之间深度融通、文科与理工农医交叉融合，融入现代信息技术赋能文科教育，实现自我的革故鼎新，新文科建设势在必行。"学科英语是外语学科和专业学科相互交叉、彼此融合的产物，符合国家"新文科"建设的时代愿景。开辟外语学科建设的全新思路，是当前外语教学改革的重要突破方向。

"中国科学院大学研究生教材系列"将切实满足特定专业学生群体的英语学习需求作为教材编写的重要依据，充分考虑到具体学习者群体的学习目标和学习诉求，具有以实际应用为导向的根本特质。该系列教材不仅关注教材编写前期的需求分析，同时重视教材试用阶段使用者的实际反馈，因为我们认为，直面使用者反馈是确定教材价值的关键一环，是重新审视学习者需求的宝贵机会，更是反复改进教材质量的可靠抓手。

"中国科学院大学研究生教材系列"融入现代信息技术，运用语料库的数据处理方法，整理归纳学科英语的语言特点和语篇特征。语料库方法可以十分客观快捷地捕捉学术语篇中的词汇、短语、搭配、语块、句子结构等语言层面的使用规律，正在成为学术和学科英语研究领域新近涌现的热点之一。然而，语料库技术运用于教材编写的尝试却寥寥无几，该系列教材无疑为语料库方法运用于教材编写做出了开创性的贡献。语料库的运用不仅能够呈现自然学术语境中真实的语言使用，更为重要的是，能够引导学习者建立适合自己微观研究方向的专业文献语料库，并将其作为未来学术生涯的开端以及追随学术生命成长过程的见证。学科英语语料库一方面可以成为研究者文献阅读经历不断累积的记录，另一方面也可能成为研究者写作不竭的灵感源泉和他们未来指导学生进行专业写作的宝贵财富。基于学科英语语料库的教材建设在"授人以鱼"的同时也在"授人以渔",而学习者也会因此获得"授人以渔"的能力。

我们正处在一个教育变革的时代。新的时代呼唤符合国家发展需求的教育理念和新颖实用的教学方法,同时也鼓励教师队伍努力探索新型的教材编写模式。"中国科学院大学研究生教材系列"积极响应时代的要求,是国家"新文科"建设指导思想下的勇敢尝试。

该系列教材的出版得到中国科学院大学教材出版中心资助,在此表示感谢。

高　原

2022 年 5 月

前　言

根据《学位与研究生教育发展"十三五"规划》的指导精神，我国研究生教育需要推进世界一流大学和世界一流学科建设，努力提高研究生参与各类国际学术交流活动的主动性与活跃度，加快培养能参与国际事务的高层次专门人才。中国科学院大学外语系自2016年起，分步骤在大学本科、硕士研究生、博士研究生三个学习阶段，对原有的通用英语课程进行学术英语课程改革。改革后，博士研究生阶段的课程为"学科学术英语"。由此，《学科英语写作教程：地学》一书开始编写。

本书的编写主要基于近几年的地学重点期刊论文及地学论文语料库，选材真实、专业性强，贴近研究热点，全面反映了地学学科学术英文论文的写作范式。本书共七章，围绕学术英语论文中标题、摘要、引言、方法、结果、讨论、总结与致谢的写作规范展开。每章的主体内容由整体概述、案例分析、功能句型、时态分析、重要语法点等板块构成，个别章节会根据单元主题做出相应调整。其中，"重要语法点"板块依次在每章展开介词、冠词、非谓语动词、从句、衔接手法、模糊限制语、名词化等专题讲解，以更好地解决地学相关专业学生的写作痛点——容易犯语法错误、表意不清、表达不地道、缺乏写作练习等，从而帮助学生巩固语法知识，恰当使用学术写作策略，为写出高质量的英文学术论文打好基础。本书还精心设计了既注重语言能力提升又锻炼思辨能力的学术阅读与写作练习题，涵盖词语填空、选择、句子填空、文段润色、语篇提升等多种题型，旨在帮助学生全面提升其学术论文写作水平与学术思辨能力。文末还附有地学专业论文常用词汇搭配附录，能有效帮助相关专业学生尽快掌握本领域的术语搭配，提高写作的准确性与规范性。

本书适合地学相关专业的高年级本科生、硕博研究生与科研工作者使用。它既可以当作论文写作类教材，也可以当作工具参考书。在具体使用时，编者建议读者根据本书列出的语步，在平时阅读论文时继续总结相应的写作表达与句型，建立起自己的学术语料库。

由于编者水平有限，书中难免存在不足，恳请同行专家和读者朋友提出修改建议，在此表示衷心的感谢！

编　者

2022 年 10 月

Contents

Chapter 1 Titles — 1

1.1 Grammatical Constructions in Titles — 2
1.2 Using Prepositions Properly — 5
1.3 Using the Definite Article "the" Properly — 8

Chapter 2 Abstracts — 13

2.1 An Overview of the Abstract Section — 14
2.2 Useful Expressions and Sentence Patterns — 18
2.3 Verb Tenses in the Abstract Section — 23
2.4 Using Non-finite Verbs Properly — 24

Chapter 3 Introductions — 31

3.1 An Overview of the Introduction Section — 32
3.2 Useful Expressions and Sentence Patterns — 34
3.3 Verb Tenses in the Introduction Section — 37
3.4 Paraphrasing — 38
3.5 Synthesizing Sources — 39
3.6 Inserting Dependent Clauses — 41

Chapter 4 Methods — 49

4.1 An Overview of the Methods Section — 50
4.2 Useful Expressions and Sentence Patterns — 51

4.3 Verb Tenses in the Methods Section — 55
4.4 Cohesive Devices — 55

Chapter 5 Results — 65

5.1 An Overview of the Results Section — 66
5.2 Useful Expressions and Sentence Patterns — 67
5.3 Verb Tenses in the Results Section — 71
5.4 Nominalization — 72
5.5 Usages of "with" in Academic Writing — 73

Chapter 6 Discussions — 81

6.1 An Overview of the Discussion Section — 82
6.2 Useful Expressions and Sentence Patterns — 84
6.3 Verb Tenses in the Discussion Section — 88
6.4 Using Hedges — 89

Chapter 7 Conclusions and Acknowledgements — 99

7.1 An Overview of the Conclusions Section — 100
7.2 An Overview of the Acknowledgements Section — 102
7.3 Useful Expressions and Sentence Patterns — 103
7.4 Sentence Structures — 104

References — 111

Appendix I Frequently-used Collocations in Geoscience Papers — 119

Appendix II Keys to Exercises — 143

Chapter 1
Titles

1.1 Grammatical Constructions in Titles

Generally, there are four types of grammatical constructions in titles, including full-sentence, nominal group, compound, and question constructions (Hartley, 2008). The titles of most research papers in geoscience are either nominal group constructions or compound constructions. Among the following 50 titles, 26 are in nominal group constructions, and 14 in compound constructions.

A. Full-sentence constructions

* *Mg–O isotopes trace the origin of Mg-rich fluids in the deeply subducted continental crust of Western Alps*
* *Weak bedrock allows north-south elongation of channels in semi-arid landscapes*
* *Lateral H_2O variation in the Zealandia lithospheric mantle controls orogen width*
* *Deformation of mantle pyroxenites provides clues to geodynamic processes in subduction zones: Case study of the Cabo Ortegal Complex, Spain*
* *Understanding sea-level change is impossible without both insights from paleo studies and working across disciplines*

B. Nominal group constructions

* *Estimates of olivine-basaltic melt electrical conductivity using a digital rock physics approach*
* *Formation timescales of CV chondrites from component specific Hf–W systematics*
* *Glacier velocity variability due to rain-induced sliding and cavity formation*
* *A new boron isotope-pH calibration for Orbulina universa, with implications for understanding and accounting for "vital effects"*
* *Abrupt plant physiological changes in southern New Zealand at the termination of the Mi-1 event reflect shifts in hydroclimate and pCO_2*
* *Cosmogenic ^{22}Na as a steady-state tracer of solute transport and water age in first-order catchments*
* *Creep strength of ringwoodite measured at pressure-temperature conditions of the lower part of the mantle transition zone using a deformation-DIA apparatus*
* *Eastern Indian Ocean microcontinent formation driven by plate motion changes*
* *Influence of the Amazon River on the Nd isotope composition of deep water in the western equatorial Atlantic during the Oligocene–Miocene transition*
* *The effects of magmatic processes and crustal recycling on the molybdenum stable*

* isotopic composition of Mid-Ocean Ridge Basalts
* Two-phase deformation of lower mantle mineral analogs
* Complementary element relationships between chondrules and matrix in Rumuruti chondrites
* Continental climate gradients in North America and Western Eurasia before and after the closure of the Central American Seaway
* Evidence for a dynamic East Antarctic ice sheet during the mid-Miocene climate transition
* Hinterland drainage closure and lake formation in response to Middle Eocene Farallon slab removal, Nevada, U.S.A.
* Immediate propagation of deglacial environmental change to deep-marine turbidite systems along the Chile convergent margin
* Seasonal variations in dissolved neodymium isotope composition in the Bay of Bengal
* Slow fault propagation in serpentinite under conditions of high pore fluid pressure
* The neodymium stable isotope composition of the silicate Earth and chondrites
* Changes in the occurrence of extreme precipitation events at the Paleocene–Eocene thermal maximum
* Timescale of overturn in a magma ocean cumulate
* Thermal-chemical conditions of the North China Mesozoic lithospheric mantle and implication for the lithospheric thinning of cratons
* Testing Late Cretaceous astronomical solutions in a 15-million-year astrochronologic record from North America
* Surface and subsurface hydrology of debris-covered Khumbu Glacier, Nepal, revealed by dye tracing
* Predicted diurnal variation of the deuterium to hydrogen ratio in water at the surface of Mars caused by mass exchange with the regolith
* Magma interactions, crystal mush formation, timescales, and unrest during caldera collapse and lateral eruption at ocean island basaltic volcanoes (Piton de la Fournaise, la Réunion)

C. Compound constructions

* Cenozoic paleoaltimetry of the SE margin of the Tibetan Plateau: Constraints on the tectonic evolution of the region
* Linking subsurface to surface degassing at active volcanoes: A thermodynamic model with applications to Erebus volcano
* Lu–Hf geochronology on cm-sized garnets using microsampling: New constraints

on garnet growth rates and duration of metamorphism during continental collision (Menderes Massif, Turkey)
* Conodont (U–Th)/He thermochronology: A case study from the Illinois Basin
* Absence of thermal influence from the African Superswell and cratonic keels on the mantle transition zone beneath southern Africa: Evidence from receiver function imaging
* Dissolved and particulate ^{230}Th–^{232}Th in the Central Equatorial Pacific Ocean: Evidence for far-field transport of the East Pacific Rise hydrothermal plume
* River network evolution as a major control for orogenic exhumation: Case study from the western Tibetan Plateau
* Exhumation history of the West Kunlun Mountains, northwestern Tibet: Evidence for a long-lived, rejuvenated orogen
* P-wave velocity structure beneath Mt. Melbourne in northern Victoria Land, Antarctica: Evidence of partial melting and volcanic magma sources
* Active fault system across the oceanic lithosphere of the Mozambique Channel: Implications for the Nubia-Somalia southern plate boundary
* Constraints on the timing and duration of orogenic events by combined Lu–Hf and Sm–Nd geochronology: An example from the Grenville orogeny
* Geomorphic evidence for the geometry and slip rate of a young, low-angle thrust fault: Implications for hazard assessment and fault interaction in complex tectonic environments
* The influence of seawater calcium ions on coral calcification mechanisms: Constraints from boron and carbon isotopes and B/Ca ratios in Pocillopora damicornis
* Melting experiments on the Fe–C binary system up to 255 GPa: Constraints on the carbon content in the Earth's core

D. Question constructions

* How do machine learning techniques help in increasing accuracy of landslide susceptibility maps?
* Simulating rotating fluid bodies: When is vorticity generation via density-stratification important?
* Rupture speed and slip velocity: What can we learn from simulated earthquakes?
* A ~9 Myr cycle in Cenozoic $\delta^{13}C$ record and long-term orbital eccentricity modulation: Is there a link?
* Epeirogeny or eustasy? Paleozoic–Mesozoic vertical motion of the North American continental interior from thermochronometry and implications for mantle dynamics

Based on the above 50 titles, some tips on how to write a good title can be summarized. Firstly, you should be cautious with using articles and prepositions. Titles rarely begin with the article "the". In the titles listed above, only three of them begin with "the", i.e., "The effects of magmatic processes and crustal recycling on the molybdenum stable isotopic composition of Mid-Ocean Ridge Basalts", "The neodymium stable isotope composition of the silicate Earth and chondrites", and "The influence of seawater calcium ions on coral calcification mechanisms: Constraints from boron and carbon isotopes and B/Ca ratios in Pocillopora damicornis". Also, prepositional phrases are widely used in titles, so make sure that you use prepositions correctly.

Secondly, you are not allowed to use full stops in titles. None of the above titles contains a full stop, even though some of them are full sentences. A compound construction title consists of two parts which are separated by a colon, and the first letter of the first word in the second part should be capitalized, even if the first word is an indefinite article, such as "Constraints on the timing and duration of orogenic events by combined Lu–Hf and Sm–Nd geochronology: An example from the Grenville orogeny".

Lastly, you should use modifiers properly. In the titles listed above, before or after a noun or a noun phrase, there are often some modifiers. They can either be prepositional phrases, such as "in subduction zones", "during the Oligocene–Miocene transition", and "before and after the closure of the Central American Seaway", or non-finite verbs, including "using a deformation-DIA apparatus", "using a digital rock physics approach", and "caused by mass exchange with the regolith". Using modifiers properly can make titles informative, specific, and distinctive, as they can reveal the site of your research or the novel method used in your research. Editors and readers will not be attracted by titles that are too general or do not convey any intriguing information.

1.2 Using Prepositions Properly

In this part, types of prepositions, functions of prepositional phrases, and collocations containing prepositions are introduced to help writers of research papers have a better understanding of how to use prepositions properly.

1.2.1 Types of Prepositions

A. Simple prepositions, such as "about", "at", "through", "of", "since", etc.

* *Although linear increases **of** ^{230}Th concentrations **with** depth are observed **at** both **of***

our sites **from about** 0 to 2,000 m, ...
* Cyclic voltammograms (CVs) were performed **in** an N_2-saturated 2mM Fe(II) solution amended **with** 1mM **of** the various Me(II) **at** room temperature **at** a scan rate **of** 50 mV/s.
* Open system melt generation **within** a short time period would have had to be followed **by** focused channeling **of** the extracted mantle-derived melts **through** a crustal conduit.
* Temperature profiles were taken **with** a thermistor probe near the deepest point **in** each lake, and several measurements **within** the metalimnion **of** the stratified lakes allowed precise calculation **of** the depth **of** the thermocline—taken **as** the plane **of** the maximum rate **of** decrease **in** temperature.
* The next step was to filter the correlograms to enhance the signal-to-noise ratio **by** applying a singular value decomposition-based Wiener filter.

B. Compound prepositions, such as "into", "onto", etc.

* The combined effect of wider and faster propagating dykes allows greater volumes of magma to flow **into** the host rock surrounding the magma chamber.
* The recovered rare earth fraction was dried down, redissolved in 0.18 M HCl, and loaded **onto** a second cation exchange column containing 0.6 mL of Eichrom™ LN spec resin of particle size 50 μm to 100 μm.

C. Double prepositions, such as "until after", "from among", etc.

* No tornado warning was issued **until after** the tornado lifted.
* We have chosen NRI **from among** the several available metrics for phylogenetic diversity.

D. Phrasal prepositions, such as "according to", "because of", "in spite of", etc.

* Grayscale subvolumes were processed **according to** the procedure detailed in Miller et al. (2014) to remove noise and artifacts, improving the efficacy of automatic segmentation algorithms.
* Dust affects the planet's radiative balance **because of** its role in the albedo.
* **In spite of** the fact that Maori and Pacific movers have an equal number of UZs with high CVD rates in the Q4 highly deprived quartile, the geography of CVD for Pacific movers reveals very different patterns than those observed among Maori.

E. Participle prepositions, such as "regarding", "concerning", "including", "given", etc.

* We thank G. Gaetani and E. Sarafian from Woods Hole Oceanographic Institution (WHOI) for their insight **regarding** water content in mantle minerals and melts.

> * Unfortunately, data **concerning** the interactions of all species modeled in this work does not exist at relevant P–T conditions.
> * The model considers all possible sources of fluid from multiple depths, **including** degassing of dissolved volatiles during crystallization and/or decompression.
> * This is unlikely **given** that only a few percent of Hypatia is non-carbonaceous material.

1.2.2 Functions of Prepositional Phrases

In academic writing, a prepositional phrase is frequently used as an attribute or adverbial. Some examples are shown below.

A. Used as an attribute

> * Cores were imaged using a combination of absorption-contrast and phase-contrast X-ray μ-CT at 27 keV to resolve the small density contrast **between olivine and basaltic glass**.
> * An open-flow gas exchange system (LI-6800, LI-COR, U.S.A.) was used to measure leaf gas exchange in the newest fully expanded flag leaf **at the filling stage**.

B. Used as an adverbial

> * **With the enforcement of** the projects of agricultural land retrieval to forest and grassland, a large area of farmland would be restored to grasslands or forests.
> * **In the Transantarctic Mountains**, the Ferrar is intruded into the mostly terrestrial Devonian to Triassic sedimentary deposits of the Beacon Supergroup.

1.2.3 Collocations Containing Prepositions

Writers are advised to acquire collocations containing prepositions and use them correctly in academic writing. Some examples are shown below.

A. Preposition + noun + preposition

> * However, the resulting succession of laminated crusts (thick red layer **at the bottom of** the snowpack in Fig. 7) was easily observable during field campaigns throughout the season.

B. Verb + preposition

> * All of these models **focus on** constraining chemical equilibrium between a single melt and fluid.

C. Adjective + preposition

> * The result of the model run is a list of possible combinations of gases and their proportions that, when combined, are **equal to** the composition of gas measured at the surface.

You can use online corpuses to confirm the correctness and accuracy of the collocations used in your academic papers when you are not sure about their usages. Some corpuses are recommended such as SKELL, Corpus of Contemporary American English (COCA), Just the Word, etc. Do not coin strange collocations that are not accepted by native English speakers.

1.3 Using the Definite Article "the" Properly

It is not easy for writers to use the definite article "the" in scientific writing. How to use it will be introduced in this part. Generally speaking, "the" can be used to refer to the following five aspects.

A. Something mentioned in the preceding sentence

> * In Nancy, noble gases and **nitrogen** were extracted conjointly in samples H-N$_1$, H-N$_2$, and H-N$_3$ upon heating in high-vacuum with an infra-red (IR) CO$_2$ laser...**The nitrogen** was purified in a glass line.
> * In Paris, the nitrogen content and isotope composition of **two Hypatia diamond samples** were investigated...**The two samples** were weighed before their analysis.

B. A particular area

> * ...such as **the Kuiper Belt**, where presolar components might be more abundant.
> * ...in **the southwestern side** of the Libyan Desert Glass strewn field.
> * ...in **the Central Equatorial Pacific Ocean** (~155°W–159°W) at two sites.
> * **the** Batavia and Gulden Draak microcontinents
> * **the** Perth Abyssal Plain
> * **the** Asteroid Belt
> * **the** Sahara
> * **the** Persian Gulf
> * **the** Black Forest
> * **the** Iberian Peninsula

C. Something unique

* *the* Pacific
* *the* Earth
* *the* equator
* *the* Nile
* *the* North Pole

D. A particular noun/method/pattern/model

* *the* lattice parameter refined from the X-ray diffraction pattern
* *the* $^3He/^4He$ ratios
* *the* model calculations by Leya & Masarik (2009)

E. A nominalization

* *the* presence of contaminants and important amounts of water
* *the* release of some atmospheric Ne
* *the* right side of pure potential end-members
* *the* addition of some cosmogenic ^3He
* *the* isotopic spectra of Xe

Remember, do not use "the" before: (1) names of continents, such as Asia, Africa, etc.; (2) names of most countries/territories, such as Japan, Mexico, Singapore, except for the Netherlands, the United States, etc.; (3) names of cities, towns, or states, such as Tokyo, New York, Miami; (4) names of lakes and bays, such as Lake Titicaca, Lake Tanganyika, except for a group of lakes like the Great Lakes; (5) names of mountains, such as Mount Qomolangma, Mount Fuji, except for the ranges of mountains like the Rockies; and (6) names of islands, such as Isles of Scilly, except for the island chains like the Aleutians.

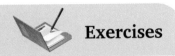

I. Fill in the following blanks with appropriate prepositions.

1. Glacier longitudinal profiles _____ regions of active uplift

2. Constraints _____ crystal storage timescales in mixed magmas: Uranium-series disequilibria in plagioclase from Holocene magmas at Mount Hood, Oregon

3. A new hydrothermal scenario _____ the 2006 Lusi eruption, Indonesia: Insights from gas geochemistry

4. Waveform tomography imaging _____ a megasplay fault system in the seismogenic Nankai subduction zone

5. Spin transition _____ ferric iron in Al-bearing Mg-perovskite up to 200 GPa and its implication _____ the lower mantle

6. _____ 2012–2014, we measured Na and ^{22}Na in precipitation _____ Williamsburg, which is on the Coastal Plain geologic province of Virginia.

7. Five-liter samples _____ varying depths (24.5–4,601m) were collected.

8. Each Cubitainer was rinsed with trace metal grade acid (10% HCl), cleaned three times _____ Milli-Q water, air-dried in a laminar airflow hood and stored separately inside the clean laboratory of the R.

9. Voxel (3D pixel) values in the reconstructed images roughly correspond _____ material density.

10. Samples often exhibit significant decompression cracking. These cracks are voids that are not present _____ elevated pressure and temperature.

II. Fill in the following blanks with correct articles or zero article.

Paragraph One

^{230}Th ($t_{1/2}$ = 75.69 kyr) is widely used as **1.** _____ quantitative marine geochemical tracer due to its highly reactive chemical behavior. It is produced by **2.** _____ radioactive decay of ^{234}U, which is conservative in seawater and has a long residence time (~200 kyr; Henderson & Anderson, 2003). ^{230}Th is essentially insoluble in seawater, so as it is produced, it is quickly removed from the water column by **3.** _____ adsorption onto particles which then settle to the seafloor. This process of adsorption and removal of ^{230}Th from **4.** _____ water column is called scavenging. ^{230}Th concentrations in seawater provide insights into **5.** _____ oceanographic processes such as deep oceanic circulation and mixing rates, and marine particle dynamics. In addition, ^{230}Th studies of marine sediments provide **6.** _____ important information on **7.** _____ past changes in fluxes to **8.** _____ seafloor, which can be used to better understand **9.** _____ climate-related changes in **10.** _____ marine biological productivity, dust input to the oceans, and deep water circulation once the systematics are adequately understood. (Lopez, 2015)

Paragraph Two

Using **1.** _____ revised protocol of **2.** _____ GEOTRACES program, radionuclide measurements of total and dissolved ^{230}Th and ^{232}Th were evaluated. **3.** _____ water samples were weighed and spiked with ^{229}Th for isotope dilution analysis. To induce Fe(OH)$_3$ precipitation, **4.** _____ purified Fe-carrier solution (FeCl$_3$) was added. The iron chloride was purified by back extraction with isopropyl ether. After addition of the ^{229}Th spike and the FeCl$_3$ to the seawater sample, it was left to equilibrate for a day before the addition of trace metal-grade NH$_4$OH to bring the pH to 8–8.5. Once at desired pH, removal of all Th and precipitation of iron hydroxide/Fe(OH)$_3$ within the seawater sample was achieved. **5.** _____ sample was left to equilibrate for five days, so **6.** _____ precipitate was able to settle undisturbed at **7.** _____ bottom of the Cubitainer. After five days, the precipitate was separated from the supernatant solution through siphoning into 1 L acid-washed Nalgene bottles, and left to equilibrate for a full day. **8.** _____ following day, **9.** _____ sample was siphoned into **10.** _____ acid-washed 50 mL centrifuge tubes, and placed in a centrifuge at 1,700 rpm for 15 minutes. Samples were centrifuged three times, decanting the supernatant each time before dissolving the precipitate in ultrapure HNO$_3$. The resulting solution was then evaporated in an acid-washed 15 mL Savillex beaker. Once evaporated, the sample was reconstituted in ^{8}N HNO$_3$. (Lopez, 2015)

Chapter 2
Abstracts

2.1 An Overview of the Abstract Section

An abstract is an overview of a research paper. It appears at the beginning of the paper. It can begin with introducing background information, identifying the gap(s) in previous studies, or stating your study purpose(s) or the assumption(s) you have tested. Also, it may explicitly or implicitly give information about your study methods, findings, and implications (Hartley, 2008). The sequence of the elements mentioned above is not strictly specified. You are advised to include the necessary elements required by your target journal. Four typical case studies are as follows.

↪ Case Study One

Excerpt (Iacovino, 2015)	Comments
Abstract ① Volcanic plumbing systems are the pathways through which volatiles are exchanged between the deep Earth and the atmosphere. ② The interplay of a multitude of processes occurring at various depths in the system dictates the composition and quantity of gas eventually erupted through volcanic vents. ③ Here, a model is presented as a framework for interpreting surface volcanic gas measurements in terms of subsurface degassing processes occurring throughout a volcanic plumbing system. ④ The model considers all possible sources of fluid from multiple depths, including degassing of dissolved volatiles during crystallization and/or decompression as recorded in melt inclusions plus any co-existing fluid phase present in a magma reservoir. ⑤ The former is achieved by differencing melt inclusion volatile contents between groups of melt inclusions saturated at discrete depths. ⑥ The latter is calculated using a thermodynamic model, which computes the composition of a C–O–H–S fluid in equilibrium with a melt given a minimum of five thermodynamic parameters, commonly known for natural systems (T, P, fO$_2$, either fH$_2$ or one parameter for H$_2$O, and either fS$_2$ or one parameter for CO$_2$). ⑦ The calculated fluids are thermodynamically decompressed and run through a mixing model, which finds all possible mixtures of subsurface fluid that match the chemistry of surface gas within ± 2.0 mol%. ⑧ The method is applied to Mount Erebus (Antarctica), an active, intraplate volcano whose gas emissions, which emanate from an active phonolitic lava lake, have	**Background:** Sentences ①② **Methodology:** Sentences ③–⑩

(Continued)

Excerpt (Iacovino, 2015)	Comments
been well quantified by FTIR, UV spectroscopy, and multi-gas sensors over the last several decades. ⑨ In addition, a well-characterized suite of lavas and melt inclusions, and petrological interpretations thereof, represent a wealth of knowledge about the shallow, intermediate, and deep parts of the Erebus plumbing system. ⑩ The model has been used to calculate the compositions of seven C–O–H–S fluids that originate from four distinct regions within the Erebus plumbing system and in the lava lake (deep basanite, intermediate, shallow phonolite, and lava lake phonolite equilibrium fluids, plus crystallization-induced degassing of deep, intermediate, and shallow melts). ⑪ A total of 144 possible mixtures were found.	**Results:** Sentences ⑪–⑬
⑫ In all cases, ~60% of the surface gas is sourced from deep degassing. ⑬ The remaining ~40% is made up primarily of fluid in equilibrium with the lava lake (~20%) plus intermediate (~10%) and phonolite (~5%) equilibrium fluids and minor to no contribution from all other fluid sources. ⑭ These results, whereby the surface gas signature is dominated by fluids originating from deep mafic melts, could be representative of any volcanic system comprised of a deep mafic member and shallow evolved fractionates as has been inferred at Yellowstone, Etna, and many others. ⑮ At Erebus, results of this modeling demonstrate that the degassing of stagnant magma can contribute significant fluid and energy to the system such that the continuous convection and degassing of volatile-rich magma is not necessary to explain the volcano's persistently active nature or the composition of its gas emissions.	**Implications:** Sentences ⑭ ⑮

▸ Case Study Two

Excerpt (Morison, 2019)	Comments
Abstract	
① The formation and differentiation of planetary bodies are thought to involve magma oceans stages. ② We study the case of a planetary mantle crystallizing upwards from a global magma ocean. ③ In this scenario, it is often considered that the magma ocean crystallizes more rapidly than the time required for convection to develop in the solid cumulate. ④ This assumption is appealing since the temperature and composition profiles resulting from the crystallization of the magma ocean can be used as an initial condition for	**Background:** Sentence ① **Purpose:** Sentence ② **Assumption:** Sentences ③ ④

(Continued)

Excerpt (Morison, 2019)	Comments
convection in the solid part. ⑤ We test here this assumption with a linear stability analysis of the density profile in the solid cumulate as crystallization proceeds. ⑥ The interface between the magma ocean and the solid is a phase change interface. ⑦ Convecting matter arriving near the interface can therefore cross this boundary via melting or freezing. ⑧ We use a semi-permeable condition at the boundary between the magma ocean and the solid to account for that phenomenon. ⑨ The timescale with which convection develops in the solid is found to be several orders of magnitude smaller than the time needed to crystallize the magma ocean as soon as a few hundreds kilometers of cumulate are formed on a Mars to Earth-size planet. ⑩ The phase change boundary condition is found to decrease this timescale by several orders of magnitude. ⑪ For a Moon-size object, the possibility of melting and freezing at the top of the cumulate allows the overturn to happen before complete crystallization. ⑫ The convective patterns are also affected by melting and freezing at the boundary: The linearly most-unstable mode is a degree-1 translation mode instead of the approximately aspect-ratio-one convection rolls found with classical non-penetrative boundary conditions. ⑬ The first overturn of the crystallizing cumulate on Mars and the Moon could therefore be at the origin of their observed degree-1 features.	**Methodology:** Sentences ⑤–⑧ **Results & Discussion:** Sentences ⑨–⑬

▸ Case Study Three

Excerpt (Whittaker et al., 2016)	Comments
Abstract ①The roles of plate tectonic or mantle dynamic forces in rupturing continental lithosphere remain controversial. ② Particularly, enigmatic is the rifting of microcontinents from mature continental rifted margins, with plume-driven thermal weakening commonly inferred to facilitate calving. ③ However, a role for plate tectonic reorganizations has also been suggested. ④ Here, we show that a combination of plate tectonic reorganization and plume-driven thermal weakening was required to calve the Batavia and Gulden Draak microcontinents in the Cretaceous Indian Ocean. ⑤ We reconstruct the evolution of these two microcontinents using constraints from new paleontological samples, $^{40}Ar/^{39}Ar$ ages, and	**Gap:** Sentences ①–③ **Results:** Sentences ④⑥⑦ **Methodology:** Sentence ⑤

Chapter 2
Abstracts

(Continued)

Excerpt (Whittaker et al., 2016)	Comments
geophysical data. ⑥ Calving from India occurred at 101–104 Ma, coinciding with the onset of a dramatic change in Indian plate motion. ⑦ Critically, Kerguelen plume volcanism does not appear to have directly triggered calving. ⑧ Rather, it is likely that plume-related thermal weakening of the Indian passive margin preconditioned it for microcontinent formation, but calving was triggered by changes in plate tectonic boundary forces.	**Discussion:** Sentence ⑧

➥ Case Study Four

Excerpt (Stewart et al., 2016)	Comments
Abstract	
① Dissolved and particulate neodymium (Nd) are mainly supplied to the oceans via rivers, dust, and release from marine sediments along continental margins. ② This process, together with the short oceanic residence time of Nd, gives rise to pronounced spatial gradients in oceanic $^{143}Nd/^{144}Nd$ ratios (ε_{Nd}). ③ However, we do not yet have a good understanding of the extent to which the influence of riverine point-source Nd supply can be distinguished from changes in mixing between different water masses in the marine geological record. ④ This gap in knowledge is important to fill because there is growing awareness that major global climate transitions may be associated not only with changes in large-scale ocean water mass mixing, but also with important changes in continental hydroclimate and weathering. ⑤ Here, we present ε_{Nd} data for fossilized fish teeth, planktonic foraminifera, and the Fe–Mn oxyhydroxide and detrital fractions of sediments recovered from Ocean Drilling Project (ODP) Site 926 on Ceara Rise, situated approximately 800 km from the mouth of the River Amazon. ⑥ Our records span the Mi-1 glaciation event during the Oligocene–Miocene transition (OMT; ~23 Ma). ⑦ We compare our ε_{Nd} records with data for ambient deep Atlantic northern and southern component waters to assess the influence of particulate input from the Amazon River on Nd in ancient deep waters at this site. ⑧ ε_{Nd} values for all of our fish teeth, foraminifera, and Fe–Mn oxyhydroxide samples are extremely unradiogenic ($\varepsilon_{Nd} \approx -15$); much lower than the ε_{Nd} for deep waters	**Background:** Sentences ①② **Gap:** Sentence ③ **Significance:** Sentence ④ **Results:** Sentences ⑤⑥⑧ **Methodology:** Sentence ⑦

(Continued)
Excerpt (Stewart et al., 2016)	Comments
of modern or Oligocene–Miocene age from the North Atlantic ($\varepsilon_{Nd} \approx$ –10) and South Atlantic ($\varepsilon_{Nd} \approx$ –8). ⑨ This finding suggests that partial dissolution of detrital particulate material from the Amazon ($\varepsilon_{Nd} \approx$ –18) strongly influences the ε_{Nd} values of deep waters at Ceara Rise across the OMT. ⑩ We conclude that terrestrially derived inputs of Nd can affect ε_{Nd} values of deep water many hundreds of kilometers from source. ⑪ Our results both underscore the need for care in reconstructing changes in large-scale oceanic water-mass mixing using sites proximal to major rivers, and highlight the potential of these marine archives for tracing changes in continental hydroclimate and weathering.	**Discussion:** Sentences ⑨–⑪

2.2 Useful Expressions and Sentence Patterns

Useful expressions and sentence patterns used in different elements of the Abstract section are as follows.

A. Introducing the characteristics of a substance

* *Raman spectroscopy is a kind of molecular fingerprint spectrum, which **has been widely used in the field of** material composition identification and quantitative analysis.*
* *The gas distribution area **is characterized by** high resistivity anomaly.*
* *Boron isotope ratios, as measured in planktic foraminifera, can **be a useful tracer of** past ocean pH.*
* *Moreover, this kind of reductant **has proven to be effective in** remediating HOCs contaminated wastewaters.*
* *Agricultural reclamation **has been the major threat to** land use changes.*
* *The use of prefabrication for building **has many benefits, including** improved construction process efficiency.*
* *Suitable straw returning to field technology **is not only beneficial to** maintain soil fertility, **but also** to reduce environmental pollution caused by straw burning.*
* *High-temperature stable isotope fractionations can **provide important insights into** the nature and conditions of the processes involved in planetary differentiation.*
* *This **is composed primarily of** ~70% volume (Mg, Fe)SiO$_3$ bridgmanite and ~25%*

volume (Mg, Fe)O ferropericlase.
* **The two major components of** *carbonaceous chondrites* **are** *chondrules and matrix.*
* **They were deformed** *in the D-DIA at 5 GPa and 800–1000 °C, with MgO accommodating the majority of strain.*
* *Ordinary chondrites (OC), as well as enstatite chondrites (EC),* **have very low matrix fractions***.*
* *The group of Rumuruti chondrites (R chondrites)* **is chemically and isotopically related to** *OC and EC.*

B. Introducing the relationship between two variables

* *Deposits* **are typically associated with** *specific magma types formed by melting of sedimentary rocks.*
* *Seepage activity is a complicated hydro geology process that* **is mainly correlated with** *hydrate formation.*
* **There is a positive exponential correlation between** *the maximum detection resistivity and the gas ejection velocity.*
* *Some studies suggested that biomass-based ratios of fungus to bacteria* **are positively correlated to** *ecosystem efficiency and food web complexity.*

C. Establishing the importance of a research topic

* *Studying the response characteristics of submarine cold seepage bubble plumes* **is of great significance to** *determine the gas hydrate reservoir area.*
* *The acid properties of SAPO-34 molecular sieves (MSs), including the strength and density of Brönsted acids,* **have attracted enormous attention** *in past decades because of the excellent performance of SAPO-34 in industrial processes.*
* *How to analyze quantitatively the results obtained by comprehensive control benefit of soil erosion for well instructs of the soil and water conservation work* **is a topic worthy of a long-term study** *in southern China.*
* **Understanding** *arc magma genesis* **is critical to** *deciphering the construction of continental crust.*
* **It is important to further investigate** *this composition* **using another approach***.*
* *We notably present some examples of bathymetric data and seismic lines showing these structures and we* **discuss the significance of** *this fault system in the plate tectonics framework of the East African offshore.*

D. Identifying the gap in previous studies

* *But the extent of reported carbon reductions achieved through prefabrication remains inconsistent,* ***it is still unclear*** *how different variables influence a prefabricated building's LCCa.*
* *However, the effects of substructure variance in manganese oxide on the adsorption sites and adsorption characteristics* ***remain unclear****.*
* *Over the past decades, extensive marshlands had been converted to paddy fields in the Sanjiang Plain, China; however, the effect of this land use change on ecosystem carbon budget* ***is still much uncertainty****.*
* *However,* ***there has been little to no empirical evidence that*** *elucidates the greenhouse gas (GHG) emissions from this method.*
* *However, the acoustic velocity model* ***cannot describe the physical properties of****..., and the acoustic wave equation adopted* ***is not applicable for*** *the numerical simulation of high frequency seismic waves.*
* *These studies represent an important knowledge base but they* ***do not cover*** *the required spatial range and time-frame.*
* *So far, only few microstructural studies of natural pyroxenites* ***have been carried out****.*
* *The principal characteristics of the continental rise* ***which have not previously been explained*** *are: the persistent uniformity in morphology, sediment…*

E. Introducing the focus, aim, or argument of a research paper

* ***The intention here is to*** *approach the problem by examining Cenozoic examples of subduction initiation.*
* ***This paper focuses on*** *a review of the in-situ measurement of cold seep.*
* ***Our study is centered on*** *the high-resolution post-glacial tephrochronological record for Mocho-Choshuenco volcano.*
* ***The aim of this paper is to investigate*** *the detailed characteristics of the upper mantle discontinuities above 400 km depth.*
* *We make the database publicly available,* ***intending to provide*** *the seismological and broader scientific community* ***with a benchmark for*** *time series to be used as a testing ground in signal processing.*

F. Explaining the significance of the present study

* ***By applying this understanding to*** *the optimization of fracturing designs for the Longmaxi shale, we* ***successfully created*** *networks of well-propped fractures.*
* *Considered together with the mapping objectives,* ***these products are an important***

and accessible way for geologists without a technical background in machine learning *to* interrogate the results of supervised bedrock prediction.
* **Our dye tracing experiments have revealed previously unknown features** of the subsurface hydrology of a Himalayan debris-covered glacier.
* **Our observations are notable due to** the style and magnitude of the forcing (high rain rates).
* **The experiments highlight the role of** biotite and of crystallization pressure in defining separate compositional trends of residual liquids, i.e., alkaline (trachytes) versus sub-alkaline (dacite-rhyolite).
* **The potential applications of** this data collection **are innumerable**: from recalibrating fragility curves to training machine learning models to quantifying earthquake damage.
* **These analyses enable us to precisely** constrain the age of the sediments, **accurately** locate the sources of the deposits, and **place robust constraints on** the exhumation and magmatic history of the West Kunlun Mountains.
* **Our study will contribute to a better understanding of the influence of** climate change and increasingly serious human disturbances.
* **Our results provide new insights into** the synergistic effects of CTAB on dehalogenation of Cl-OPEs.
* **Our study provides the effective means** of land use dynamic monitoring.

G. Introducing the study methods briefly

* *Here, we **present** a new open-ocean calibration of the planktic foraminifera Orbulina universa.*
* *Here, we **examine** glacier speed and rain-induced accelerations using...*
* *To explore how these wetland ecosystems respond to such environmental changes, we **examined the effect of** saline-alkaline stresses and water stress (flooding/drought) on water use efficiency.*
* *Here, we **investigate** the ^{230}Th and ^{232}Th depth profiles in the Central Pacific Basin.*
* *We **used** a combination of synchrotron X-ray fluorescence and high-resolution electron microprobe element mapping to compare...*
* *This study **assessed** carbon budget changes to...*
* *Here, a model **is presented** as a framework for interpreting surface volcanic gas measurements.*
* *To monitor volcanic activity and glacial movements near Jang Bogo Station, a seismic network **was installed** during the 2010–2011 Antarctic summer field season.*
* *To navigate this complexity, mafic magma diversity **is investigated using** sample suites that span short temporal and spatial scales.*

* *In this study, land use and landscape pattern changes from 1982 to 2015* ***were analyzed using*** *remote sensing data...K-means clustering of different rainstorm patterns* ***was used to*** *differentiate watershed run-off and sedimentation features.*

H. Reporting the results briefly

* ***The results of*** *TG and Rietveld refinement* ***showed that****...*
* *The amount of plastic litter* ***has increased dramatically*** *over the last few decades in both aquatic and terrestrial environments.*
* *The software provides the inversion parameters (FDS asymptotes) as well as the limiting frequency effect and transition factor, which* ***provide information regarding*** *contribution of the SP particles to magnetic susceptibility as well as relative variation of the particle grain-size in the SP-SSD transition.*
* *Then, the obtained area under curve* ***values*** *(AUCs)* ***were obtained between*** *0.90 (in 360.009 s)* ***and*** *0.84 (in 78.307 s).*
* *Moreover,* ***an increase in*** *density, through biofouling by organisms, can* ***eventually result in*** *sinking of microplastics.*
* *Besides,* ***it is found that there is a correlation between*** *chlorine resistance and antibiotic resistance.*

I. Showing explanations for research results

* *This* ***is attributed to*** *greater preservation of the enriched melt signature arising from reactive melt transport within the mantle wedge.*
* ***Due to errors in*** *experimental procedures, we did not collect data for approximately nine samples (indicated by Table 1).*
* *Most of this difference* ***is due to*** *the greater water depth and, hence, larger inventory of ^{230}That the 8°N site.*
* *Dissolution of dust is the main source of dissolved ^{232}Th to the CEP* ***because of*** *its remoteness from the continental margins.*

J. Discussing the implications of the research

* *The results* ***indicated that*** *the largest reduction of forestland area was 648.70 km^2 during 1995–2000, and the relative change was −1.84%.*
* *At Erebus, results of this modeling* ***demonstrate that*** *the degassing of stagnant magma can contribute significant fluid and energy to the system.*
* *Finally, the factors limiting the application of Raman spectroscopy in deep sea are summarized, which can* ***provide reference for the future development of*** *Raman*

spectroscopy technology.

* *The cavity modification via incorporating zinc ions effectively tunes the product selectivity over SAPO molecular sieves with relatively larger cavity, which **provides a novel strategy to** develop…*
* *The research results will **provide theoretical support for** the planning and design of cascade hydropower stations in tributaries of the Yangtze River as well as operation of the Three Gorges Reservoir.*
* *The results **suggested that** the NDVI alone was not able to distinguish drought-related vegetation stress from vegetation changes caused by crop rotation between corn and soybeans.*
* *Our model **has important implications for** arc magma genesis in general.*

2.3 Verb Tenses in the Abstract Section

A. Background information: Simple present tense

* *The dynamics of magmatic processes at large mafic ocean island volcanoes **control** the likely locations (central caldera versus flanks) and timing of their eruptions.*

B. Purpose: Simple present tense / Simple past tense

* *Here, we **report** the results of sixteen fluorescent dye tracing experiments conducted in April–May 2018 over the lowermost 7 km of the high-elevation, debris-covered Khumbu Glacier, Nepal, to characterize the glacier's surface and subsurface drainage system.*
* *The research **aimed to** take peat land of Changbai Mountain area as research object.*

C. Gaps in previous studies: Simple present tense

* *However, the FORC signal of particles with nonuniform magnetizations, which are the main carrier of natural remanent magnetizations in many systems, **is** still poorly understood.*
* *Crystals and their melt inclusions **are** key witnesses of these processes but **are** rarely **studied** in detail and in the same samples.*

D. Methods: Simple present tense / Simple past tense

* *Here, we **use** a coupled atmosphere-ocean general circulation model, HadCM3L, to*

> study regional changes in metrics for extreme precipitation across the onset of the PETM by comparing simulations performed with possible PETM and pre-PETM greenhouse gas forcing.
> * We **analyzed** seven sediment cores recovered from marine turbidite depositional sites along the Chile continental margin.

E. Results: Simple present tense / Simple past tense

> * Monitoring data **show** that inflation of the edifice **started** about a month before the first 2007 eruption: Magma intrusion **occurred** at ≈ 3 km below sea level, and quickly **migrated** towards shallower depths (about 1 km above sea level).

F. Conclusions/Implications: Simple present tense / Modal auxiliaries

> * Our findings **emphasize** that the eastern branch of East African Rift System is extending largely towards the south, not only in continental domains but also through the oceanic lithosphere of the Mozambique basin.
> * We **conclude** that turbiditic strata **may constitute** reliable recorders of climate change across a wide range of climatic zones and geomorphic conditions. However, the underlying causes for similar signal manifestations in the sinks **may differ**, ranging from maintained high system connectivity to abrupt connectivity loss.

2.4 Using Non-finite Verbs Properly

Different from a finite verb, a non-finite verb is a verb form that does not show the tense. Also, it is inflected for neither number nor person, so it is never the main verb (the predicate) in a sentence. Different types of non-finite verbs are introduced as follows.

A. Infinitives: to + verb

> * **To address** this simultaneity (endogeneity) problem, this paper proposes the use of the IV-GMM technique.
> * Another way **to determine** the Mo stable isotope composition of the BSE is **to use** recent oceanic basalts.

B. Participles: Present participle / Past participle

> * Acceleration events correspond with times when bed separation also increases

> rapidly, **indicating** that the acceleration...
> * Hydrocarbon seepage erupts along a fault to seabed as bubbles and oil drops, **releasing** a large amount of hydrocarbons.
> * This episode of exhumation and uplift, **associated** with magmatism across western Tibet, is compatible with a double-sided lithospheric wedge model.

C. Gerunds: Verb + ing

> * ***Understanding*** such riverine processes together with their spatial and temporal changes is central to the understanding of landscape evolution in the Himalayas.
> * ***Quantifying*** the dust flux is challenging.

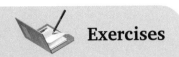

Exercises

I. Identify the non-finite verbs in the following sentences.

1. Here, we examine glacier speed and rain-induced accelerations using a near-continuous 26-month-long GNSS time series from a large maritime glacier (Tasman Glacier, New Zealand).

2. The short-term accelerations are superimposed on longer-term periods of enhanced velocity that persist for days to weeks and decay at similar rates to bed separation estimates and proglacial lake levels.

3. Accelerated exhumation of the mountain front at a rate of ~1.1 km/Myr since ~15 Ma supports active compressional deformation at the margins of the northwestern Tibetan Plateau.

4. Polycyclic aromatic hydrocarbons (PAHs) in 35 peat samples collected from the Mildred peat core in the Athabasca Region, Canada, were quantitatively analyzed by gas chromatograph mass spectroscopy (GCMS).

II. Read the following paragraphs and find out the four errors contained in the underlined sentences. Each underlined sentence contains only one error. In each case, only one word is involved. You should proofread the sentences and correct the errors.

1. <u>Tibet, the highest and widest plateau on Earth, usually described as a high-elevation, low-relief geomorphic feature.</u> However, relief (i.e., elevation difference between the highest and lowest points in a given area) is not uniform cross the plateau, with distinct morphological contrast between different parts of Tibet.

2. <u>Central Tibet has the lowest relief compare to the rest of the plateau, likely because it is internally drained (Fig. 1a) and has low precipitation rates (Liu-Zeng et al., 2008).</u> The internal drainage favors low relief because of internal deposition, which tends to smooth topography. 3. <u>Areas has significant relief (> 2 km) are limited to active rifts, such as the Nyainqentanglha range.</u> Early studies (Shackleton & Chang, 1988) suggest that low relief formed in central Tibet from Middle to Late Miocene and corresponds to an erosion surface. However, for northern central Tibet (Qiangtang block), Rohrmann et al. (2012) suggest that 4. <u>a transition from a fast to slow exhumation regime, similar to the modern one, occurring during Late Cretaceous–Early Cenozoic times.</u> Haider et al. (2013) reconstruct a similar exhumation history for the southern part of central Tibet (Lhasa block), and using thermochronology; Hetzel et al. (2011) suggest that the low-relief surface on the northern Lhasa block formed before 50 Ma. In addition, paleo

elevation studies imply that central Tibet was already near its present elevation by Late Eocene. Thus, modern elevation and relief in central Tibet might have been reached by 45 Ma. (Gourbet et al., 2016)

III. In the following paragraph, some sentences are missing. Fill in the blanks with the most suitable ones from the list A–F. There are two extra choices, which do not fit in any of the gaps.

Regolith on Mars exchanges water with the atmosphere on a diurnal basis and this process causes significant variation in the abundance of water vapor at the surface. **1.**_____ We are therefore motivated to investigate isotopic water exchange between the atmosphere and the regolith and determine its effect on the deuterium to hydrogen ratio (D/H) of the atmosphere. We model transport of water in the regolith and regolith-atmosphere exchange by solving a transport equation including regolith adsorption, condensation, and diffusion. **2.**_____ The fractionation in adsorption is caused by the difference in the latent heat of adsorption, and that of condensation is caused by the difference in the vapor pressure. Together with a simple, bulk-aerodynamic boundary layer model, we simulate the diurnal variation of the D/H near the planetary surface. **3.**_____ The variability is mainly driven by adsorption and desorption of regolith particles, and its diurnal trend features a drop in the early morning, a rise to the peak value during the daytime, and a second drop in the late afternoon and evening, tracing the water vapor flow into and out from the regolith. The predicted D/H variation can be tested with in-situ measurements. **4.**_____ (Hu, 2019)

A. The model calculates equilibrium fractionation between HDO and H_2O in each of these processes.

B. We find that the D/H can vary by 300‰–1400‰ diurnally in the equatorial and midlatitude locations, and the magnitude is greater at a colder location or season.

C. The adsorbed water is released to the atmosphere and re-adsorbed to the regolith on a diurnal basis.

D. While previous studies of regolith-atmosphere exchange focus on the abundance, recent in-situ experiments and remote sensing observations measure the isotopic composition of the atmospheric water.

E. As such, our calculations suggest stable isotope analysis to be a powerful tool in pinpointing regolith-atmosphere exchange of water on Mars.

F. On Earth, measuring the isotopic composition of water near the surface is a common way to identify the sources of boundary layer water.

IV. There are four blanks in each paragraph below, only one of which needs to be filled in with a missing sentence. Fit the following two sentences into the best positions.

A. *We ascribe this subdued effect to a transition zone around the magma chamber, which is still solid rock but with relatively low Young's modulus due to high temperatures.*

In geodynamic numerical models of volcanic systems, the volcanic basement hosting the magmatic reservoir is often assumed to exhibit constant elastic parameters with a sharp transition from the host rocks to the magmatic reservoir. **1.**_____ We assess this assumption by deriving an empirical relation between elastic parameters and temperature for Icelandic basalts by conducting a set of triaxial compression experiments between 200°C and 1,000°C. **2.**_____ Results show a significant decrease of Young's modulus from ~38 GPa to less than 4.7 GPa at around 1,000°C. Based on these laboratory data, we develop a 2D axisymmetric finite-element model including temperature-dependent elastic properties of the volcanic basement. As a case study, we use the Snæfellsjökull volcanic system, western Iceland to evaluate pressure differences in the volcanic edifice and basement due to glacial unloading of the volcano. First, we calculate the temperature field throughout the model and assign elastic properties accordingly. Then, we assess unloading-driven pressure differences in the magma chamber at various depths in models with and without temperature-dependent elastic parameters. **3.**_____ With constant elastic parameters and a sharp transition between basement and magma chamber, we obtain results comparable to other studies. However, pressure changes due to surface unloading become smaller when using more realistic temperature-dependent elastic properties. **4.**_____ We discuss our findings in the light of volcanic processes in proximity to the magma chamber, such as roof collapse, dyke injection, or deep hydrothermal circulation. Our results aim at quantifying the effects of glacial unloading on magma chamber dynamics and volcanic activity. (Bakker et al., 2016)

B. *The location of the plate boundaries is well-defined along the continental branches of the EARS which include a western branch and an eastern branch (Fig. 1).*

The East African Rift System (EARS), originally described by Suess (1891), corresponds to the northern part of the divergent plate boundary system between the Nubian (West African) and Somali (East African) plates. **5.**_____ This rift system is connected northward to the Afar hot spot which is related to the opening of the Red Sea and the Gulf of Aden, which began being active about 30 Ma ago. **6.**_____ However, it is considered that the EARS began to be active only later, starting 24 Ma ago in the Afar area. Although the EARS is commonly considered as the modern archetype of rifted plate boundaries, the current Nubia–Somalia kinematics is among the least well-known of all the major plate boundaries. **7.**_____ The plate boundary between Nubia and Somalia developed over thousands of kilometers across the eastern part of Africa during Late Oligocene and Neogene times. **8.**_____ The eastern branch (Gregory Rift) is characterized by high volcanic activity (including Mount Kilimanjaro, the highest point of Africa) and the western branch (Albertine Rift) is characterized by a moderate volcanic activity relative to the eastern branch and by deeper basins, containing lakes and sediments. (Deville et al., 2018)

Chapter 3
Introductions

3.1 An Overview of the Introduction Section

According to Swales & Feak (2004), three moves should be included in the Introduction section. Writers of research papers can follow the moves to write a proper introduction.

- **Move 1: Establishing a Research Territory**

  - by showing the importance of the topic;
  - by reviewing previous studies.

- **Move 2: Establishing a Niche**

  - by indicating a gap in previous studies.

- **Move 3: Occupying the Niche**

  - by stating the purpose of new research;
  - by raising research questions / listing the hypothesis to be tested;
  - by reporting major findings.

Two typical case studies are as follows.

Case Study One

Excerpt (Chen et al., 2016)	Comments
Introduction ① Fluids are important for mass transfer in subduction zones. ② Arc volcanics are commonly characterized by enrichment of large ion lithophile elements (LILE) and light rare earth elements (LREE) relative to the high field strength elements (HFSE) and heavy rare earth elements (HREE). ③ This geochemical feature is generally attributed to slab-derived fluids, which transfer the characteristic signature from subducting slabs to arc volcanics via metasomatism of the mantle wedge. ④ However, it is usually tricky to trace fluids from different sources, especially those from dehydration of serpentinite. ⑤ Coesite-bearing whiteschist at Dora-Maira in the Western Alps is characterized by enrichment in Mg but depletion in Na, Ca, Fe^{2+}, and LILE relative to the host metagranite. ⑥ This provides an excellent target to study	**Prior knowledge:** Sentences ①–⑥

Chapter 3
Introductions

(Continued)

Excerpt (Chen et al., 2016)	Comments
the fluid-rock interaction in a typical continental subduction zone. ⑦ Although intensive studies have been devoted to the whiteschist since the first discovery of coesite in it, its petrogenesis is still a matter of hot debate. ⑧ The controversy mainly focuses on the timing and mechanism of Mg enrichment… ⑨ Resolving the metasomatic timing and the source of metasomatic fluids in whiteschist petrogenesis can shed new light on fluid-rock interaction in subduction zones and its effect on the geochemistry of deeply subducted crustal rocks. … ⑩ In this contribution, we present an integrated study of whole-rock Mg and O isotopes, and zircon U–Pb ages and O isotopes for whiteschist and its host rock from Dora-Maira. ⑪ The new results, integrated with previous data, shed new light not only on the origin of Mg-rich fluids for whiteschist formation in Western Alps but also on fluid-rock interaction in the continental subduction channel.	**Gaps in previous studies:** Sentences ⑦⑧ **Significance of the present study:** Sentences ⑨–⑪

➪ Case Study Two

Excerpt (Geng et al., 2019)	Comments
Introduction ① Cratons, the Archean cores of continents, are normally underlain by thick (> 200 km), old, and cold lithospheric roots that persist for billions of years. ② It is traditionally thought that the negative thermal buoyancy of the cold cratonic lithosphere is largely balanced by the positive chemical buoyancy due to the depletion in iron by extensive melt extraction… ③ However, the dramatic influence of volatiles, especially water, on mantle rheology has been challenged by recent laboratory experiments, which suggest only a small effect of water on upper mantle rheology. ④ Therefore, the preservation of cratonic roots for billions of years and the mechanisms of their later remobilization require more investigation. … ⑤ Unfortunately, due to the rarity of mantle xenoliths, direct information from the lithospheric mantle during this period is sparse. ⑥ Mantle-derived primitive magmas, however, provide another important window to decipher the thermal-chemical conditions of the lithospheric	**Prior knowledge:** Sentences ①② **Gaps in previous studies:** Sentences ③–⑥

Excerpt (Geng et al., 2019)	Comments
mantle. ⑦ Here, we present combined whole-rock chemical, Sr–Nd–Pb isotopic compositions and mineral chemistry of two suites of Early Cretaceous primitive basalts from the western Liaoning Province in the eastern NCC and use them to constrain the thermal-chemical conditions of the Mesozoic lithospheric mantle beneath the eastern NCC. ⑧ We provide key evidence to help explain how the Archean lithospheric mantle of the eastern NCC has been removed.	**Significance of the present study:** Sentences ⑦⑧

3.2 Useful Expressions and Sentence Patterns

Useful expressions and sentence patterns used in different moves of the Introduction section are as follows.

A. Establishing the importance of a research topic

* *Understanding the processes that occur in the magma plumbing system below ocean island volcanoes and how they relate to monitoring data, **are key current topics of research** because they can lead to improved volcanic hazard assessment.*
* *As such, they **have been the subjects of numerical studies** aimed at relating the behavior of individual magnetic particles and small assemblages to experimental bulk properties.*
* *Consequently, the viscosity of ringwoodite **is critical for** understanding the mantle dynamics in and around the MTZ.*
* *Thus, **it is fundamental to** take into account this mechanism on modeling.*
* *Therefore, **it is vital to** explore leaf margin conditions of woody dicots.*
* *Both problems **are of great importance** for calibration and for parameters retrieval.*
* *Constraining the nature of these building blocks of Earth **is important**, because...*
* *Habitat connectivity **is a key issue in** landscape ecology...*

B. Defining terms

* *The X method **is a valuable tool** used to...*
* *A landslide **is defined as** the movement of a mass of rock...*
* *Our heuristic method relies on another measurement **referred to as** "cumulative cost" of a path...*

* *Western Anatolia is composed of several metamorphic zones* (**collectively referred to as** *the Anatolides*)...

C. Referring to previous studies

* **With the exceptions of** *Pike & Fernandez (1999), Carvallo et al. (2003), and Roberts et al. (2017),* **all of these numerical studies have concentrated on** *FORC diagrams.*
* **Several authors have proposed** *the presence of a dominantly oceanic Lwandle block...extending south of the Rovuma block in the Mozambique Channel between southern Mozambique and Madagascar* **(Hartnady, 2002; Horner-Johnson et al., 2007; Stamps et al., 2008, 2018; Saria et al., 2014)**.
* **Previous studies have mainly focused on** *the influence of...*
* **Previous studies determined that** *water surface slopes increased and...*
* **Previous studies have indicated that** *low-flow stages considerably decreased...*
* **Previous studies showed that** *surface water may have been continuously transported...*
* **Previous study suggested that** *soil food webs were longer and more complex...*
* **Previous studies demonstrated that** *Oribatida mites performed important functions...*
* **Numerous geodynamical studies have investigated** *the coupled evolution of Earth's interior...*
* **There is a growing body of literature on** *the geologic distinction between lakes and...*
* *...***is situated within a growing body of literature*** *within human geography.*
* **It has been shown that** *the effect of any given land-management measure...*
* *When available,* **it has been observed that** *the quality report is not always...*
* *Researchers have pointed out that* **several studies have found that** *dementia patients are at...*

D. Referring to what other writers do

* *Carvallo et al. (2003)* **used a** *finite-difference* **model to** *calculate FORC distributions for SV magnetite particles.*
* *Visser & Both (2005)* **argue that** *these mismatches may provide a necessary...*
* *Mayer et al. (2006)* **claim that** *a completeness of at least 60%...*
* *While* **Guimond & Simard (2010) assert that** *while rural researchers...*
* *Indeed,* **Oliver et al. (1999) suggested that** *leaching of the U-rich...*
* *Fyffe et al. (2019)* **also conducted a** *dye tracing* **study on** *a debris-covered glacier in the Italian Alps (Miage Glacier)...*

E. Identifying the gap in previous studies

* ...labor market integration, however, **remains unanswered**.
* Despite this conceptual knowledge, predicting sliding velocities from effective pressure **remains problematic**.
* The cause of these artefacts **has not been investigated**.
* Second, **there has been very little research about** the relationship between glacial...
* In addition, **very little research has been undertaken to understand** the potential...
* However, **there is very little research on** assessing for resilience, resulting in...
* **Few studies have simulated** future bank erosion responses to climate...
* The reality is that **few studies have justified** the added expense of analyzing such...
* **A few studies have estimated** some socio-economic impacts of the drought...
* **Only a few studies have quantified** multi-temporal glacier shrinkage for...
* Yet, **relatively few studies have applied this tool to** trace Earth surface...
* It may seem surprising that **so few studies have analyzed**...
* Yet, **few studies have focused specifically on** the cause/effect relationships between...
* **Few studies have attempted to** combine both datasets for...
* However, **few studies have investigated the application of** integrated...
* The onset time of the early Yanshanian magmatism in Southeast China **is still controversial**.
* The scheme has achieved wide use **but several issues remain unaddressed**.
* **This work did however not investigate** the emissions generated during utilization in cast-iron stoves and **this study aims to fill this gap in the current literature**.
* In contrast, the biomarkers of these Jurassic sediments **have been paid little attention**.
* In contrast, **there is no such a level of knowledge of** the Cuenca and Valencia domains.

F. Stating the purpose and significance of the present study

* Here, **we investigate..., and explore** the effects of...on...
* **The paper investigates** how territoriality influences the actor relations in...
* **In this paper, we aim to better comprehend and discuss** oasis formation...
* **Instead, we aim to provide a broad overview of** the possibilities...
* **In this study, we examine the** petrogenesis and geological **significance of**...
* **We focus on..., and compare it with**...
* **The intention here is to approach the problem by examining**...
* **The hope is that a focus on** simple models and the clearest examples will encourage...
* **The obtained results in the present study are expected to provide further insights for**...
* Integration of stratigraphy and geochemistry **gives further insights into...and helps**

evaluate...
* Thus, ***further studies are needed to resolve such an argument****...*
* ***This study attempts to provide additional information based on*** *coccoliths and* ***to build a more accurate*** *stratigraphic **framework for**...*
* ***In addition to addressing these questions,*** *we **extend** our classification scheme by...*
* *The present study **was performed in an attempt to**...*
* *This paper **presents**...and **uses this dataset to constrain**...*
* *In this study, **comprehensive analyses of**...**have been conducted on**...*
* *The **aims are to determine**..., **constrain**..., and **shed new lights on**...*

3.3 Verb Tenses in the Introduction Section

A. Introducing the characteristics of a substance: Simple present tense / Present perfect tense / Simple future tense

* *FORC diagrams **are** a powerful tool in rock magnetic studies...*
* *****It has been observed*** *that coupled $\delta^{18}O$ and $\delta^{34}S$ values of modern pore-water sulfate at different depths in marine sediment cores **will bear** a typical slope of > 0.70 where microbial dissimilatory sulfate reduction is dominated by organotrophic sulfate reduction (OSR).*

B. Establishing the importance of a research topic: Simple present tense / Present perfect tense

* *With this in mind, it **is** important to assess whether a link between permeability and electrical conductivity **is** physically justified.*
* *The supraglacial hydrology of debris-covered glaciers **has received** increasing attention in recent years.*

C. Referring to previous studies: Present perfect tense / Simple past tense / Simple present tense

* *Previous studies **have revealed** that hypoxia in bottom water...*
* *Previous studies **determined** that water surface slopes increased and...*
* *****There is*** *a growing body of literature making the connection between...*

D. Referring to what other writers do: Simple past tense

* *****Embry et al. (2013) proposed*** *that each erosional sequence boundary was generated*

> *during a brief tectonic episode lasting ⩽ 2 Myr.*
> * **Lorant et al. (1998) *introduced*** *the residence time as another key factor controlling isotopic fractionation of generated gases in conventional hydrocarbon reservoirs.*
> * **Schandl et al. (1989) *identified*** *several conditions of rodingitization and subdivided the rodingites into three groups characterized by increasing metamorphic grade.*

E. Referring to areas of inquiry: Present perfect tense / Simple past tense

> * *Recently, studies of both modern and ancient environments associated with significant SD-AOM **have revealed** a distinctively lower $\delta^{18}O$–$\delta^{34}S$ slope...*
> * *Experimental studies on nano-patterned arrays of SV particles **found** that FORC diagrams are significantly more complex than for SD signals.*

F. Identifying the gap in previous studies: Simple present tense / Present perfect tense

> * *However, the genesis of A-type granites **is** still a matter of debate.*
> * *However, a precise understanding of...**has been** under debate for a few decades.*

G. Stating the purpose and significance of the present study: Simple present tense / Modal auxiliaries

> * *Our study **provides** the effective means of land use dynamic monitoring and...*
> * *It **can** provide the reference for wetland ecosystem, especially ecosystem service...*

3.4 Paraphrasing

A paraphrase is a statement that expresses your own interpretation of important information and ideas expressed by someone else in a new form. To appropriately paraphrase, you can follow the steps below:

- read the original text until you understand its exact meaning, and then set it aside;

- write down the main points or necessary details by your short-term memory;

- change the structure of the original text by rearranging the order of sentences;

- replace keywords within the sentences with synonyms or phrases with similar meanings;

- compare your paraphrase with the original text to ensure you have not unintentionally plagiarized.

Some examples of paraphrase are shown below:

- **Original version:** *Coral calcification is a complex biological process, many aspects of which remain poorly understood (Giri et al., 2019).*

  Plagiarized version: *Coral calcification is a complicated biological process, many aspects of which remain poorly understood.*

  Paraphrased version: *Our understanding of coral calcification, a complex biological process, is limited. (Giri et al., 2019)*

- **Original version:** *Another way to determine the Mo stable isotope composition of the BSE is to use recent oceanic basalts (Bezard et al., 2016).*

  Plagiarized version: *An alternative method for determining the Mo stable isotope composition of the BSE is to use recent oceanic basalts.*

  Paraphrased version: *Recent oceanic basalts can be used to determine the Mo stable isotope composition of the BSE. (Bezard et al., 2016)*

3.5 Synthesizing Sources

Synthesizing is distinct from summarizing, as writers summarize key information of one or more sources without making comments or providing new insights. When synthesizing, writers can not only synthesize multiple sources but also express their attitudes towards the sources, based on which they can make new conclusions.

There are five widely-used ways for synthesizing sources, including synthesizing sources grouped by classification, by the order from distant to close, by the order from earliest to latest, by making comparison and contrast, and by giving examples. In addition to using them separately, writers can synthesize sources by combining these ways appropriately.

A. Sources grouped by classification

The following excerpt synthesizes the previous sources by introducing different methods to measure the creep strength of ringwoodite.

- ***The creep strength of ringwoodite was measured by*** *the in-situ stress-strain measurements at 21–23 GPa and 1,800 K by using a rotational Drickamer apparatus (RDA) with synchrotron X-ray...*

> ***The creep strength of ringwoodite was also measured to 10 GPa at room temperature by** the in-situ stress-strain measurements using a deformation-DIA (D-DIA) apparatus with synchrotron X-ray. (Kawazoe et al., 2016)*

B. Sources ordered from distant to close

The following excerpt begins with introducing the function of hinterland lakes, then introduces a problem with hinterland lakes, and next focuses on the hinterland of the North American Cordillera. In this way, the authors narrowed down the topic gradually.

> - *Hinterland lakes can accumulate archives of orogenic landscapes that are otherwise largely erosional and thus rarely preserved in the geologic record. Lacustrine lithofacies in particular can be sensitive indicators of local and regional basin hydrology, and can record subtle deformation caused by dynamic or isostatic processes. Due to structural deformation in orogenic belts and the often dynamic paleogeography of terrestrial depositional environments, hinterland lake strata are often difficult to reconstruct using traditional stratigraphic correlation. The hinterland of the North American Cordillera underwent contraction from the Triassic through Late Cretaceous due to viscous coupling between the subducting Farallon plate and North American lithosphere. (Smith et al., 2017)*

C. Sources ordered from earliest to latest

The following excerpt synthesizes the citations by introducing the development of relevant theories and models.

> - *Following the increase in digital terrain models (DTMs) availability **in the 1960s**, the underlying theories and mathematical developments of modern geomorphometry (i.e., based on quantitative measurements rather than qualitative observations derived from DTMs) started to be developed **in the early 1970s**. These methods and algorithms were gradually automated **in the 1980s** as computers became more available. (Lecours et al., 2016)*

D. Sources ordered by making comparison and contrast

The following excerpt synthesizes the previous studies with similar findings. The linking word "Similar" connects the two findings.

- *The pioneering study of AvéLallemant was amongst the first to explore the deformation processes in natural websterites and to highlight their complexity. It showed that under high temperature conditions (i.e., above 1,050°C), the deformation of the volumetrically dominant clinopyroxene (cpx) is mostly accommodated by dislocation creep through non-selective translation gliding, polygonization, and syntectonic recrystallization, while at lower temperatures, mechanical twining is more common.* **Similar** *conclusions were reached by Kirby and Kronenberg who observed dominance of kink bands and twinning at low temperatures and a switch to subgrain rotation and recrystallization at temperature higher than 1,000°C. (Henry et al., 2017)*

The following excerpt synthesizes the sources by introducing what will happen when the glacier substrate is hard or soft.

- ***When the glacier substrate is hard***, *the reduction in effective pressure caused by increasing basal water pressure has a direct effect on sliding velocity by reducing ice-bed contact and increasing zones of cavitation.* ***When the glacier substrate is soft and deformable****, reducing the effective pressure reduces the shear strength of the substrate, and may result in enhanced sliding at the top of the substrate and enhanced deformation at depths of decimeters to meters within the substrate. (Horgan et al., 2015)*

E. Sources ordered by giving examples

The following excerpt uses the Papatea fault in the northern South Island as an example to demonstrate that young faults can be difficult to identify.

- *Young faults can have little stratigraphic offset and subtle geomorphic expression, which makes them difficult to identify prior to earthquake rupture and can, therefore, be overlooked in seismic hazard assessments.* ***For example,*** *the Papatea fault in the northern South Island, New Zealand, is a recently identified, structurally immature fault with small stratigraphic offset that potentially enhanced fault connectivity and increased earthquake magnitude during the 2017 Mw 7.8 Kaikoura earthquake. (Hughes et al., 2018)*

3.6 Inserting Dependent Clauses

A dependent clause has a subject and a verb, and it has to be attached to an independent clause (Fadlalla, 2019). Inserting a dependent clause into an independent one appropriately can increase your sentence variety, thus improving the language quality of your research papers. Common types of dependent clauses are as follows.

A. Attributive clauses

* The pre-Jurassic U–Pb age spectrum is strikingly similar to those from Triassic sediments in the eastern Pamir and Songpan-Ganzi terrane **that were interpreted to have close affinity**.
* The lower 10 km of Tasman Glacier is covered in debris (0–3 m thick, or greater) and the glacier terminates in a proglacial lake **that began to form in 1985 and covered 6.7 km^2 by May 2013 (Fig. 1)**.

B. Non-restrictive / Non-defining attributive clauses

* This article is based on hydrological and sediment monitoring data from 2002 to 2016 of four important hydrological control stations set up in the main tributaries of the Yangtze River, **which are Tongzilin, Gaochang, Beibei, and Wulong**.
* Furthermore, cascade hydro power stations were built, **which led to annual average sediment concentration, annual sediment load, median size of sediment, and modulus of sediment transport to decrease by 5%~79.34%**.
* There are few exceptions on the relationships between precipitation, floods, and sediment load in individual tributary basins, **which are often accompanied by a significant reduction in run-off and sediment yields**.

C. Object clauses

* The results **show that the river sediment distribution pattern and time change are almost consistent with vegetation variation characteristics and human activities**.
* The results **indicated that the precipitation and the maximal 30 minutes rainfall intensity were the most relevant factors to run-off and sediment responses**.
* In combination with the occurrence of synorogenic sediments on both flanks of the Kunlun terrane, these data **suggest that an ancient West Kunlun range had emerged above sea level by Triassic–Early Jurassic times**.

D. Appositive clauses

* This is due to **the fact that forestry and agricultural areas can easily be converted into areas of commerce and light industry**.
* To achieve this, the surfaces need to represent 2D dimensional probability distributions and therefore need to fulfil **the requirement that the volume underneath each surface is equal to 1**.

E. Adverbial clauses

* ***If the peak ages show little change up section***, *a situation known as a static peak, the source terrain likely experienced rapid cooling at the time corresponding to the peak ages, but exhumed slowly since then.*
* *In this case, zircon double dating allows identifying volcanogenic zircon **when its crystallization age (e.g., zircon U–Pb age) is equal to the corresponding cooling age (e.g., ZFT) within error**, and thus has great potential to calibrate poorly-dated sediments in foreland basin settings.*
* *Additionally, the source areas of zircons belonging to specific age peaks can be identified **where modern bedrock ZFT ages are similar or younger**.*
* ***Since fluid travels through distinctly different pathways***, *generalization of empirical relations that link permeability and electrical conductivity lacks a microstructural justification, and should be verified case-by-case.*
* ***Although the samples are not cogenetic***, *they evolved under similar magmatic conditions.*
* ***As India's motion became more northerly***, *resisting forces along this overall plate boundary pathway (along the WZFZ and through the PAP) increased, **so that other alternative plate boundary pathways became more attractive**.*

F. Subject clauses

* *It is unlikely **that partial melting involved in the production of MORBs themselves results in a significant departure of the $\delta^{98}/^{95}Mo$ of the magma from its source**.*
* *Comparing Figs. 3c and 3e, it is clear **that the geometric structure of many voxels was misclassified using fixed sized voxels**.*

G. Predicative clauses

* *Our interpretation of the episodic pulses of MMCT IRD at Site U1356 **is that overall advance was punctuated by retreats of the ice sheet**.*
* *The fact **is that till date, not many terrestrial impacts are documented and surely, many of them may have gone unnoticed**.*

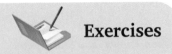 **Exercises**

I. **Integrate the following simple sentences in each segment into one that is more formal and logical.**

1. This thrust belt probably reactivated the Paleozoic Kudi suture, given their similar trace in map view (Fig. 1). This is our inference.

   _____
   _____

2. Stomatal density (SD) and stomatal index (SI) in fossil Litsea calicarioides leaves reveal large changes. These changes are coincident with the three phases identified by the carbon isotope values (Fig. 4).

   _____
   _____

3. The Antarctic Ice Sheet is estimated to have melted from ~125% to ~50% of its modern size. There is thus far no evidence for an increase in atmospheric CO_2 associated with the Mi-1 glacial termination in the earliest Miocene.

   _____
   _____

4. To the southwest, the Tianshuihai–Karakoram terranes have been sliced by the Karakorum fault. Along the Karakorum fault, the Baltoro batholith intruded at 26–15 Ma.

   _____
   _____

5. As a result, plates show a degree of coupling. These plates should share an interlocking ridge-transform plate boundary.

   _____
   _____

Chapter 3
Introductions

6. Leaf physiology and phenotype are the results of numerous environmental parameters, including Ca. This is evident.

7. Current theory concerning the leaf physiological response over millennial timescales supports our interpretation. Our interpretation is that the reduction of $g_{c[max]}$ from Phase 1 to Phase 2, and subsequent increase from Phase 2 to Phase 3 (Fig. 4), can reflect an increase in Ca during the ~20 kyr period comprising Phase 2.

8. In this case, the rift zone is small, and rifting and breakup occur relatively quickly. So, the spatiotemporal relationship between rifting and other events is potentially more easily isolated than for larger rifts between the major continents.

II. Paraphrase the following sentences.

1. The capacity of the upper mantle to transport melt, which is ultimately responsible for the production of oceanic crust, strongly depends on the spatial distribution of melt in the upper mantle.

2. The magnetotelluric (MT) method, which exploits the high conductivity of partially molten rock, is a valuable tool used to probe the melt content of the upper mantle.

3. Mountain glaciers and ice caps are anticipated to contribute significantly to sea level rise over the coming century. There are two components to this contribution: changes in surface mass balance and changes in dynamics (e.g., accelerated flow, lake, or tidewater calving).

4. Hysteresis is often observed with identical effective pressures resulting in markedly different velocities. This hysteresis was demonstrated over short time intervals by Sugiyama & Gudmundsson (2004) who observed two distinct relationships between effective pressure and glacier speed depending on whether Pe is increasing or decreasing.

_____
_____

5. The intensification of heat stress reduces the labor capacity and hence poses a threat to socio-economic development.

_____
_____

6. As an important factor influencing the local development, a growing body of studies has been focusing on the assessment of climate change impacts on the labor system, and then adapting to potential impacts.

_____
_____

III. There are four blanks in each paragraph below, only one of which needs to be filled in with a missing sentence. Fit the following four sentences into the best positions.

A. *In contrast, the exhumation histories of the northwestern plateau margin, in particular the West Kunlun Mountains (Mts.) (Fig. 1), remain poorly constrained so far, due to scarce thermochronologic data in this vast region of remote mountains.*

  1._____ Decoding mountain building processes of the Tibetan Plateau and their geodynamics requires documenting long-term orogenic scale uplift and exhumation histories. 2._____ Many areas of the orogen have well documented cooling histories constrained by dense thermochronologic datasets, such as the southern and eastern plateau margins. 3._____ As such, the onset of plateau formation in northwestern Tibet remains largely disputed, ranging from 46 Ma to 4.5 Ma. 4._____ (Cao, 2015)

B. *Based on data from the three-component stations, 17 volcanic events were roughly located.*

  The first geophysical observations at Mt. Melbourne were set up in 1988 by the Italian Progetto Nazionale de Ricerche in Antartide (PNRA) program. 5._____ A network of five tilt stations was installed in 1988–1989 for continuous recording, and a seismic network was set up in 1990 that consisted of two short-period single-component and two short-period three-component stations constrained by a local trigger. **6.**_____ The long-period features of the events may have been caused by the active presence of magmatic fluids in the source processes or the result of fracturing processes between brittle and plastic behaviors. **7.**_____ The other seismic array was operated with three-component 5-s sensors recording continuously during the austral summers of 1993–1994 and 1994–1995 in the PNRA framework. **8.**_____ Four temporary stations were located at the vertices of a square-shaped array around Mt. Melbourne, and the crustal thicknesses at each station were computed with teleseismic receiver functions (circles with crustal thickness in Fig. 1). (Park et al., 2015)

> C. *Similarly, the Rb–Sr mica ages from biotite and orthogneisses (Fig. 1B), in intrusion related contact to the metamorphic schists with a sedimentary precursor, yielded Paleocene–Early Eocene ages (~43–62 Ma), so far always considered to closely post-date the Alpine metamorphism of the basement series.*

The outcrop containing the large garnet megacrysts analyzed in this study is located inside mica schists in contact with orthogneiss featuring protolith ages around ~550 Ma (zircon U–Pb), and both lithological units are located below the Supra-Pan-African unconformity identified by Candan et al. (2011a). **9.**_____ Although the Menderes Massif as a whole has been extensively studied over the past century, its metamorphic history still remains uncertain. **10.**_____ A few petrological and geochronological studies address the effects of the Alpine overprint on Pan-African mineral assemblages and isotopic systems. **11.**_____ Published geochronologic constraints on the Alpine metamorphism are scattered between 63 Ma and 27 Ma. The Rb–Sr white mica (48–63 Ma with an average age of 56 ± 1 Ma) Ma and biotite (27–50 Ma with an average age of 35 ± 5 Ma) ages from meta-sedimentary rocks of the south-Menderes Pan-African basement were interpreted as cooling ages during Alpine metamorphism of the massif. **12.**_____ White-mica Ar–Ar analysis of paragneisses in the southwest Menderes nappe gave similar Eocene cooling ages of 43–37 Ma (Hetzel & Reischmann, 1996). More recently Catlos & Çemen (2005), reported three monazite Th–Pb ages of 47.1 ± 12.6, 44.7 ± 12.2 and 42.8 ± 7.2 Ma (2σ) from the northern part of the southern sub-massif, which were interpreted to record monazite recrystallization during decompression and extension of the Menderes massif. (Schmidt et al., 2015)

> D. *Several proxy studies of the hydrological response to the Paleocene–Eocene Thermal Maximum hyperthermal, ~56 Ma, have recently invoked changes in the occurrence of extreme precipitation events to explain observations, but these changes have not been studied for the geologic past using climate models.*

Future global warming is widely anticipated to increase the occurrence of extreme precipitation events, but such hydrological changes have received limited attention within paleoclimate studies. **13.**_____ Here, we use a coupled atmosphere-ocean general circulation model, HadCM3L, to study regional changes in metrics for extreme precipitation across the onset of the PETM by comparing simulations performed with possible PETM and pre-PETM greenhouse gas forcing. **14.**_____ Our simulations show a shift in the frequency-intensity relationship of precipitation, with extreme events increasing in importance over tropical regions including equatorial Africa and southern America. The incidence of some extreme events increases by up to 70% across the PETM in some regions. **15.**_____ While the most extreme precipitation rates tend to relate to increases in convective precipitation, in some regions dynamic changes in atmospheric circulation are also of importance. **16.**_____ Although shortcomings in the ability of general circulation models to represent the daily cycle of precipitation and the full range of extreme events preclude a direct comparison of absolute precipitation rates, our simulations provide a useful spatial framework for interpreting hydrological proxies from this time period. Our results indicate that changes in extreme precipitation behavior may be decoupled from those in mean annual precipitation, including, for example in East Africa, where the change in mean annual precipitation is small but a large increase in the size and frequency of extreme events occurs. This has important implications for the interpretation of the hydrological proxy record and our understanding of climatic, as well as biogeochemical, responses to global warming events. (Carmichael et al., 2018)

Chapter 4
Methods

4.1 An Overview of the Methods Section

In a research paper, the Methods section, also titled as Materials and Methods or Data and Methods, usually follows the Introduction section, explaining the research process and data analysis in detail. In this section, researchers need to introduce their study sites, materials, sampling measures, study procedures, variables, data analysis techniques, and other necessary information that enables readers to understand the researchers' study clearly (Hartley, 2008). In addition to the above-mentioned information, it is common for researchers to justify their study methods to increase the reliability of their papers. Two typical case studies are as follows.

↪ *Case Study One*

Excerpt (Allabar, 2018)	Comments
2. Methods 2.1 Starting Material and Capsule Preparation ① A crystal free VAD79 glass was synthesized following the protocol of Marxer et al. (2015) with additional improvement of the final cooling step: The melt was air cooled from 1873 K to a temperature nearby the glass transition (Tg) within ~1 min to inhibit crystallization. ② Then the supercooled melt was transferred into a furnace preheated to 833 K, whereupon the furnace was switched off to maintain a cooling rate of ~5 K·min^{-1} to room temperature, which successfully minimized tension induced crack formation within the glass batch. ③ Cylinders with 5 mm diameter were drilled out of the glass, cut to 6.5 mm length and ground at the edges to prevent capsule damage during pressurization. ④ One cylinder was embedded in epoxy resin and ground and polished for electron microprobe analysis (EMPA). ⑤ Successful homogenization of the anhydrous glass was confirmed by the EMPA using measurement conditions as described in Preuss et al. (2016) (SiO$_2$: 57.24%; TiO$_2$: 0.29%; Al$_2$O$_3$: 21.08%; FeO: 2.71%; MnO: 0.15%; MgO: 0.39%; CaO: 3.19%; Na$_2$O: 5.38%; K$_2$O: 9.47%; P$_2$O$_5$: 0.1%)… … 2.2 Decompression Experiments 2.3 Sample Preparation 2.4 FTIR Spectroscopy 2.5 Quantitative Determination of VND and Porosity	**Elaborating on study procedures while introducing instruments:** Sentences ①-⑤ This excerpt introduces the specific procedures involved in the study. It can be inferred from the title of each part in this excerpt that writers, instead of following a fixed structure, can structure the Methods section of their research papers in a way that fits their study.

Chapter 4
Methods

→ Case Study Two

Excerpt (Chen et al., 2016)	Comments
2. Geological Setting and Samples ① Dora-Maira (Fig. 1), together with outcrops at Gran Paradiso and Monte Rosa, constitute three Internal Crystalline Massifs within the Penninic Domain in the Western Alps. ② It is composed of Variscan crystalline basement and Triassic cover, and the former was intruded by Permian granitoids. ③ These rocks experienced high-pressure (HP) and ultrahigh-pressure (UHP) eclogite-facies metamorphism during the Alpine orogeny. …	Introducing study sites and samples: Sentences ①–③
3. Analytical Methods ④ Magnesium isotopes were measured using a Thermo Scientific Neptune Plus MC-ICPMS followed the method of An et al. (2014) at the CAS Laboratory of Crust-Mantle Materials and Environments in University of Science and Technology of China, Hefei. ⑤ Whole-rock powders were fully digested to obtain ~20 μg Mg for chemical purification. ⑥ A mixture of concentrated HF-HNO$_3$ was used for digestion…	Elaborating on study methods and procedures: Sentences ④–⑥

4.2 Useful Expressions and Sentence Patterns

Useful expressions and sentence patterns used in different elements of the Methods section are as follows.

A. Introducing the features/basic information of a substance/landscape/site

* *The main mechanisms responsible for its lithospheric thinning* **have been suggested to include**: *(1) lithospheric delamination; (2) thermal and chemical erosion; (3) weakening of the lithosphere by hydration; and (4) melt-peridotite reaction.*
* *Both sites are soil-mantled upland landscapes that* **are underlain by** *granodiorite.*
* *This site* **is covered by** *typical Mediterranean scrubs and is about two kilometers to the nearest village.*
* **As one of the oldest Archean cratons in the world**, *the North China Craton* **preserves** *crustal remnants as old as 3.8 Ga.*
* *Since the final cratonization at ~1.8–1.9 Ga by amalgamation of the eastern and western blocks, it* **remained undisturbed** *until the eruption of Ordovician (~470 Ma) kimberlites.*

51

* *This study was performed in six plantations of Chinese star anise of Guangxi Zhuang Autonomous Region, China at the Liuwan Forestry Center (**22°34′N, 109°51′E**), the Aisha sub-Forestry Center (**22°58′N, 108°20′E**) and...*
* *The SE Tibetan Plateau margin **is situated in** southeastern Tibet, Yunnan, western Sichuan, and Guizhou in southwestern China.*
* *The DPPR **is bounded by** Canada, the Red River of the North, and the Missouri River (Fig. 1).*
* *The headwaters of the Kay Lake valley **are made up of** sedimentary rocks of the Miocene Kailas Formation, and volcanic and plutonic rocks associated with the Cretaceous-Eocene Gangdise volcanic arc.*

B. Introducing the study instruments/materials/sites

* *Fused silica capillary tube (**300 μm OD, 50 μm ID; Polymicro Technologies, LLC**) was used to...*
* *Specimens **with largest dimensions of ⩽ 700 μm were placed in 1 mm Pt or NBtubes** for analysis.*
* *All the subvolumes used in direct current simulations, with the exception of those we used to assess the potential influence of H_2O, **have dimensions 280 μm × 280 μm × 280 μm**...*
* *The samples consisted of a black shale (**MAC1-4, 25 m depth**) from the Hushpuckney Shale member of the Missourian Patoka Formation, ...*

C. Justifying the study methods/steps

* *We have modeled the diffusive re-equilibration of H_2O of eight melt inclusions **using the method of** Qin et al. (1992).*
* ***Following** Di Muro et al. (2014), we **have assumed that** the largest measured concentrations have not been modified via diffusion and thus, we have used them as initial values.*
* *FORC diagrams **are constructed from** a class of partial hysteresis curves **called** first-order reversal curves (Mayergoyz, 1986).*
* *Age models of turbidite cores **are based on** published radiocarbon ages by Blumberg et al. (2008) and Bernhardt et al. (2015a).*
* *We **chose** the global eustatic sea-level curve of Lambeck et al. (2014) for comparison as it combines available records from the Pacific and the Atlantic.*
* *We **included** an additional humidity-index record based on grain-size end-member modeling (Weltje, 1997) of core GeoB7139-2 (detailed methods and interpretation in Appendix A).*

Chapter 4
Methods

D. Introducing the equations used

* To study the influence of AI on microclimates, we **use the normalized difference vegetation index, NDVI, calculated from** the intensity of the near infrared (NIR) and visible red (VIS) wavelengths: i.

$$NDVI = \frac{NIR - VIS}{NIR + VIS} \qquad (1)$$

* Lastly, the equation

$$H_T = \frac{(V_{S0} + \delta^{v_s}) \times (V_{P0} + \delta^{v_p})}{V_{P0} + \delta^{v_p} - V_{S0} - \delta^{v_s}} \times \frac{V_{P0} - V_{S0}}{V_{P0} \times V_{S0}} H_T \qquad (1)$$

is applied to convert the apparent depths (HA) into true depths (HT), **where V_{p0} and V_{s0} are the mean P- and S-wave speeds** in the layer in the standard Earth model, and δ^{v_p} and δ^{v_s} are the absolute P- and S-wave speed anomalies.

E. Describing the study methods/steps

* Nine samples from...**were analyzed** for the compositions of...and the contents of...
* 89 seawater samples **distributed over** six stations were collected...
* Calcium concentrations **were augmented through** the addition of $CaCl_2$.
* Water **was loaded into** the tube and **centrifuged to** the sealed end.
* The melt fraction of each subvolume **was calculated by** counting the number of...
* Contractions and dilations **were conducted** along all three orthogonal directions of the cubic subvolume.
* They **were carried out** on a suite of 120 post-glacial tephra samples from Mocho-Choshuenco, including 44 scoria cone samples.
* All rock samples **were crushed into** fragments 5–10 cm in diameter.
* **Shale samples were placed in** a 10% sodium hypochlorite solution for up to four weeks.
* Shales that did not completely disaggregate after this treatment **were subjected to** a 35% hydrogen peroxide solution for up to 24 hours.
* Undissolved residue **was washed and sieved to** isolate the 63–2,000 µm size fractions.
* Optical and cathodoluminescence (CL) microscopy observations of the cements in the studied extension veins **were used to** document the relative chronology of fracture stages.
* $NaMgF_3$ **was synthesized** for this study from a stoichiometric mixture of NaF and MgF_2 sintered at 750 °C (see Appendix A).
* We **subjected our samples to** rigorous cleaning.

* We **faulted** intact cores of serpentinite under conditions of high pore fluid pressure in a triaxial rock deformation apparatus.
* We only **compiled/analyzed samples** known to have erupted in post-glacial times (18 kyr) and from volcanic centers between 37°S and 45°S.
* We **acquired three samples from** depths of 25–76 m in the western Illinois Basin MAC core.
* We **applied** the n and k values of the closest bulk composition and **used** Equation (2) to solve for the cooling time (t in seconds).
* We **carried out**, as a sensitivity test, a spectral analysis **using** the control points provided by the ^{18}O record.
* We **measured** the activities of extracellular enzymes **using** assay techniques modified from Guan (1986).
* Here, we **categorize** the majoritic garnets **using** an experimentally calibrated model.
* A ClO_2 stock solution **was prepared using** the standard method 4500-ClO_2 B.
* The ClO_2 concentrations in the six aliquots **were calibrated using** the iodometric method.
* The concentrations of chlorite and chlorate **were determined using** an ion chromatography system (ICS-3000, Dionex, U.S.A.).
* Raman spectroscopy measurement **was performed using** a LabRam Aramis (Horiba Jobin Yvon) at room temperature under excitation by 532 nm laser with output power of ~0.5 mW.
* An alpha-ejection correction **is typically calculated using** the measured dimensions of the analyzed grain and assuming an appropriate grain geometry.
* In brief, ClO_2 gas **was generated by** slowly adding 20 mL of H_2SO_4 (10%, v/v) to 500 mL of a 0.5 M $NaClO_2$ solution.
* Ultrapure water **was provided by** a water purification system (Cascada I, Pall, U.S.A.).
* A simulated raw water sample **was prepared by** dissolving 3 mg/L SRNOM as C, 80 mg/L $NaHCO_3$ as $CaCO_3$, 2.0 mg/L NaBr as Br...
* A glassy carbon (GC) electrode (3.0 mm in diameter) coated with ferrihydrite **was used as** the working electrode.
* **For PCR analysis**, 1 L of spring water **was filtered through** a 0.2-μm Supor®-200 membrane filter (47 mm diameter) (Pall Life Science).
* **For quality control**, the R_2 of the standard curve as well as the amplification efficiency **were determined**, and melting curve analysis **was performed**.
* Our method bypasses the need for laser fluorination of high-Cr garnets, being instead **based on** laser fluorination of a low-Cr garnet (S0068).

Chapter 4
Methods

4.3 Verb Tenses in the Methods Section

A. Introducing the study instruments/materials/sites: Simple present tense

* The glacier **has** a well-documented, expanding area of supraglacial ponds...
* The offshore segment of the eastern branch of the EARS **is characterized** from north to south by Neogene extension tectonics over-imposed on former strike-slip structures of the Tanzanian–northern Mozambique transform margin.

B. Justifying the study methods/steps: Simple present tense

* We **use** the same samples studied by Di Muro et al. (2014).
* The analytical conditions **are detailed** in the Supplementary Material and are the same as in Albert et al. (2015).

C. Introducing the equations used: Simple present tense

* And n **is** the temperature coefficient for fluorescein $(0.0036°C^{-1})$.
* ...where u(t) **is** our observed speed time series and the background speed is a best fitting function a sin $(\omega t + \varphi) + bt + c$ (Section 3.1).

D. Describing the study methods/steps: Simple past tense / Simple present tense

* Two second-stage anvils made of cubic BN (BNS800, Sumitomo Electric Inc.) **were used** on the downstream side because of their low X-ray absorption.
* We **report** the details of the parameter values and equations used in the calculation in Supplementary Material.

4.4 Cohesive Devices

Cohesion refers to the glue that can hold elements in a research paper together. The common cohesive devices are listed as follows (Fadlalla, 2019).

A. "that"/"those" + of

* **The surface environment of** Mars is vastly different from **that of** Earth, in that the surface pressure and temperature are much lower, and the surface temperature has greater diurnal variation.

* This would produce **values of** $\delta^{11}B$ in Orbulina universa below **those of** ambient borate ion, which would suggest lowered microenvironment pH, counter to microelectron de observations.

B. "this"/"that"/"these"/"those"/"such" + noun

* Some data indicate that pH_{ECF} is increased by ~0.2–0.8 pH units relative to the surrounding seawater, while others suggest **this change** is as high or higher than ~1 pH unit.
* Regardless of the exact mechanism, each of **those mentioned above** produces pulses of IRD as part of dynamic cycles of ice advance and retreat.
* In these experiments, increases in $/Ca^{2+}/_{SW}$ did not significantly influence calcification rates but caused…To explain **these results**, we propose a mechanism by which $/CO_3^{2-}/_{ECF}$ is influenced by $/Ca^{2+}/_{SW}$.
* **Such chemical and isotopic characteristics** can, however, not be reconciled with mineral fractionation.
* However, many Red Sea fishes (and possibly other fauna) extend into the Gulf of Aden, so **that area** needs to be added to the Red Sea Province (Fig. 2).

C. "the" + noun

* Calcification rates were measured with the alkalinity anomaly method and are reported, along with a description of **the method**, in Giri et al. (2019).
* Despite **the shortcomings** outlined, Earth system models lend support to interpretations of…

D. Logical connectors

* **Although** these two studies have conflicting results, if the B/Ca_{SK} ratios measured in experiments displayed a rate-dependent response to increasing $/Ca^{2+}/_{SW}$, we would expect to see…
* **However**, even by applying a more realistic s-process, deficit of only 0.1% would result in a slope of 1.673, **while** generating an absolute change in $\varepsilon^{182}W$ of ~4.5 ε-units with respect to the terrestrial value.
* **Therefore**, no correction is necessary for samples All-C_2, All-NM_2, All-WM_3 and Vig_2, besides their anomalous ^{183}W.
* **In addition**, our reported ages overlap with the 1.7 ± 0.7 Ma chondrule formation age for H-chondrites reported by Kleine et al. (2008).
* **Additionally**, in the context of longstanding (>30 Myr) plume activity, a purely

plume-driven mechanism leaves one fundamental question.

* *Our model **starts with** a 10-m resolution lidar-derived digital elevation model and a 10-m resolution raster of spatially-distributed erosion rate.*
* *To estimate the background speed, we **first** remove 7-day asymmetric windows around all speed-up events exceeding 0.4 m d^{-1} (Fig. 5). The edited window period starts one **prior to** and ends six days **after** the peak speed.*
* ***In particular**, coupling across the WZFZ initially resisted the northward flight of India, **until** an alternative plate boundary pathway through the plume-weakened margin of Greater India became more viable.*
* ***Despite** this activity, the Batavia and Gulden Draak microcontinents remained part of the Greater India passive margin. **In contrast**, few volcanic outputs have been observed between 108–101 Ma, coeval with Batavia and Gulden Draak calving.*
* ***As a result**, plates that share an interlocking ridge-transform plate boundary show a degree of coupling.*

E. Using participles

* *Faraday cups were calibrated at the beginning of the session, **using** the inhouse calibration routine.*
* ***Combined** with approximations of typical local silicate and phosphate concentrations (from GLODAP/CARINA), monthly estimates of pH were calculated using CO_2 system, ...*

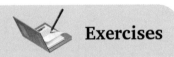
Exercises

I. Integrate the following simple sentences in each segment into one that is more formal and logical.

1. The implications of the New Mexico CAHe dates will be described in a future contribution. These implications are not discussed further here.

2. Three-dimensional images of individual conodont elements were rendered from two-dimensional attenuation slices. We did it by using the software Blob3D version 1.4.

3. We also compiled unpublished whole-rock data on basement samples. The samples were taken in the region around Mocho-Choshuenco. We did it to assess how crustal contamination may influence magma composition.

4. The magnitude of cohesion of intact serpentinite is much greater than that of plate boundary fault rocks. But the processes of crack growth and coalescence are representative of those that occur in situ. The processes of crack growth and coalescence occur in these experiments.

5. In an experiment conducted without pore fluids and in an experiment conducted at ambient temperature, axial and radial strains (a and r) were measured with foil gages. The foil gages were affixed to the surface of the rock. Axial and radial strains were used to calculate volume strain ($v = a + 2r$).

Chapter 4
Methods

6. Secondly, the studies of Kahmen et al. (2013a, 2013b) focus on open forest or scrubland plants in a highly monsoonal to arid environment. The paleoenvironment of Foulden Maar was neither monsoonal nor arid.

7. The scenario of local ecology driving physiological changes is plausible. There are several key factors why this scenario is less likely than the case for changes in pCO_2 and rainfall as drivers of variation in gc/max/, $\delta^{13}C$ and δD.

8. Dissolved deep water ε_{Nd} at these continental margin locations is likely a function of three variables. The three variables are the magnitude of the Nd flux from sediment pore fluids, the difference between the ε_{Nd} value of the overlying water and the pore fluid, and the exposure time to this benthic flux of Nd.

9. The only method is through the analysis of reductively cleaned planktonic foraminifera. By the method, ε_{Nd} values of surface waters have been successfully reconstructed to date.

10. GNSS data were processed kinematically. We did it by using differential carrier phase positioning.

11. The primary base station was also inoperable during October 2014. This leads to an increased baseline length and degraded solutions.

59

12. Understanding the causal relationship between rain-rate and velocity is complicated. We need to cross-correlate and lag the two time series.

_____

_____

II. Fill in each of the following blanks with an appropriate preposition.

We also measured Na and ^{22}Na in base flow drainage waters from Watershed 3 in the Hubbard Brook Experimental Forest (43°56′N; 71°45′W) **1.** _____ central New Hampshire, U.S.A. This watershed has been monitored for hydrologic and elemental budgets beginning in 1957 and is a member of the Long-Term Ecological Research (LTER) Network. Watershed 3 is a 42 ha catchment draining the Silurian Rangeley unit, which consists primarily **2.** _____ quartz mica schist and quartzite. Since this region was glaciated multiple times **3.** _____ the Pleistocene, thin (~1–50 cm) soils (Spodosols) are developed on till. This watershed has a total relief **4.** _____ about 60 m and is vegetated with mature northern deciduous forest dominated **5.** _____ American beech, sugar maple, yellow birch, and some red spruce **6.** _____ higher elevations. Average annual precipitation here is 1.5 m with nearly one-third of this falling as snow, and annual run-off is calculated using high-resolution (30 minutes during steady flow and six minutes **7.** _____ changing flow) gauge height (Morison, 2019). Watershed 3 has a slightly acidic pH (~6) and a relatively low dissolved load (< 2 mgL^{-1}). Given that Watershed 3 has been the hydrologic reference catchment for a wide range of paired catchment and hillslope studies for the last 50 years and has well-characterized hydrology, soils, and climate, we considered this an ideal field site **8.** _____ test ^{22}Na as a tracer. (Kaste et al., 2016)

III. There are four blanks in each paragraph below, only one of which needs to be filled in with a missing sentence. Fit the following four sentences into the best positions.

A. *Depending on how the temperature profile in the magma ocean compares with the profile of the melting temperature, two situations can occur.*

We consider a mantle that is initially fully molten and crystallizes from the bottom or some intermediate depth upward. The goal of the present study is to determine the timescale for convection to start in the solid part of the mantle as the magma ocean crystallizes. **1.** _____ For the sake of simplicity, we assume the compaction length to be small and neglect the thickness of a mush layer at the phase-change interface. **2.** _____ Matter on one side of the boundary is entirely liquid while matter on the other side is entirely solid. **3.** _____ We nonetheless allow for compositional fractionation to occur as the mantle crystallizes. The temperature at the solid/liquid boundary is denoted *Tm* and referred to as the melting temperature. **4.**_____ Either the solidification of the ocean progresses from the bottom up, or the solidification starts from an intermediate depth leading to a set-up in which the solid part of the mantle is surrounded by two magma oceans. In this second scenario, the crystallization of the surface magma ocean (SMO) is thought to be a lot faster than the crystallization of the basal magma ocean (BMO). (Morison, 2019)

> B. *After each experiment, the deformation assembly was cut in half in the plane that includes the orientation of maximum compressive stress and shear direction as presented in Fig. 3.*

Post-deformation microstructural analyses included observations using reflected light microscopy and measurements from EBSD analyses. **5.**_____ The sample was then polished using diamond lapping film with particle sizes of 30 μm down to 0.5 μm and finished by polishing for one hour with colloidal silica with a particle sizes of 0.04 μm. **6.**_____ EBSD analyses were used to measure crystallographic orientations and characterize the development of low-angle boundaries. **7.**_____ EBSD maps were made over entire cross-sections of the crystals by stitching together multiple maps using the HKL Channel 5 software. The step size used for the maps was 20 μm and the data were corrected for systematic misindexing. **8.**_____ Additional analyses, including determination of values of the Schmid factor, were carried out using the MTEX toolbox (Bachmann et al., 2010) for MATLAB®. (Tielke et al., 2016)

> C. *The fourth resonance transition test involves the AM of the ~40 kyr obliquity cycle, from which the 1.2 Myr (s4–s3) obliquity cycle should emerge.*

We follow the approach that proscribes six explicit tests to identify a resonance transition in stratigraphic data series. These tests include the assessment of amplitude modulations preserved in carrier signals (precession, obliquity, eccentricity), and the integration of these assessments with high-precision radio isotopic data. **9.**_____ The first three of the resonance transition tests involve evaluation of precession and eccentricity amplitude modulations. If the 2.4 Myr (g4–g3) eccentricity cycle is present in our stratigraphic datasets, it should ideally emerge from three "carrier signals": the AM of the shortest precession term (~19 kyr), the AM of short eccentricity (123 + 95 kyr), and the AM of the 405 kyr long eccentricity cycle. **10.**_____ A number of statistical methodologies exist for extracting these hypothesized 1.2 Myr and 2.4 Myr AMs from the higher frequency carrier signals. **11.**_____ In this study, we utilize two distinct approaches: (1) AM of the 405 kyr signal is evaluated using complex demodulation; and (2) AM of the short eccentricity (~100 kyr) and obliquity terms (~40 kyr) are conducted using time-frequency spectrum integration and a 500 kyr moving window. 12._____ The 19 kyr precession signal is not investigated in this study, given its extremely weak power in the Lisback and Iona datasets. Note that a fifth resonance transition test is the expected anti-phased relationship between short eccentricity AM and long eccentricity AM in the transition interval, which would confirm the underlying astronomical timescale. (Ma et al., 2019)

D. *We focus on the diurnal variation of the D/H of the boundary layer in this paper, because this variation may provide a direct probe of the amount and the composition of the water vapor flux between the atmosphere and the regolith.*

13._____ We construct a one-dimensional model to simulate transport of isotopic water in the Martian regolith and boundary layer. 14._____ It has a thermal diffusion module, a water transport module, and a boundary layer module. The model includes the isotope fractionation effects of adsorption, condensation, and molecular diffusion. We do not include the effects of subsurface deliquescence in this paper, and will study that subject in the future. 15._____ On a diurnal timescale, the D/H near the surface is decoupled from the effect of the large scale circulation, because the latitudinal mixing time for water is a few tens of sols. 16._____ As such we reduce the regolith-atmosphere exchange problem to a one-dimensional problem concerning the planetary boundary layer and the regolith. Except for the effects of mesoscale transport of water, our model should provide a good representation of the diurnal variability of the water abundance and isotopic composition in the boundary layer. The availability of radio isotopically dated ashes from ten biozones provides a remarkable opportunity to rigorously anchor the floating as trochronologies, and the ability to test the sensitivity of our results to timescale uncertainty (using different radioisotopic anchorings). (Hu, 2019)

IV. Improve the following paragraphs to make them more formal and logical.

1. We study both melts and crystals. We did it by employing ab initio molecular dynamics simulations based on the planar augmented wavefunctions (PAW) flavor. We used the VASP implementation. The VASP implementation has the Gamma point for sampling the Brillouin zone and generalized-gradient approximation for the exchange correlation in the PBE96 formulation. We used a kinetic energy cutoff of 550 eV for the planewave basis set, and used a kinetic energy cutoff of 800 eV for the augmentation charges. Because iron is present, all simulations which are at all volumes and temperatures are spin-polarized. This allows for the magnetic spin of the individual Fe atoms to be consistently computed at every single time step. We initiate the local magnetic moments with 1 magneton-Bohr par Fe atom. This is enough to break the symmetry of the magnetic wavefunctions that will converge to their state within a few steps.

Chapter 4
Methods

2. Phase and orientation maps of reidite-bearing zircon grains were conducted via electron backscatter diffraction (EBSD) mapping. To do it, a TESCAN MIRA3 FE-SEM at Curtin University was used. EBSD and EDS data were collected at the same time. Oxford Instruments AZtec acquisition system with a Nordlys EBSD detector and XMax 20 mm Silicon Drift Detector was used. Panchromatic cathodoluminescence (CL) and additional BSE images were collected using the same instrument. Processing of EBSD data was performed using Oxford Instruments Channel 5.12 software.

3. We use two similar metrics calculated within GB polygons to quantify topographic asymmetry. First, we collected up to 10 topographic profiles from each GB polygon. This allows their lengths to vary. This also ensures that they span the distance between opposing ridge lines and are oriented within 45° of north-south (locations of profiles provided in supplemental material). We use these profiles to compute the ratio of the average along-profile slope on north- and south-facing slopes. Second, we calculate the ratio of the average slope of gridded data measured on north- and south-facing aspects. We refer to the ratio as the average slope ratio.

4. Paleocurrents were measured previously at Kekeya. This shows that sediment provenance from the south. No such data exist at Sanju until now. We measured the orientation of 251 imbricated pebbles in the conglomerate beds along the Sanju section. We did it to obtain the paleo-flow orientation for provenance analysis. Further, we collected samples from eight fluvial sandstones interbedded with conglomerate layers at Sanju. We collected two medium-grained sandstones at Kekeya to complement our previous DZFT studies. About 50 zircon grains were randomly selected from most samples for U–Pb and fission-track double dating by Laser-Ablation ICP Mass Spectrometry (LA-ICP-MS). We made it by using the analytical parameters and procedures described in Appendix Table S1. For U–Pb ages, we only accept those data with ⩽20% discordance. Analyses are reported as $^{206}Pb/^{238}U$ ages for zircon ages ⩽1.0 Ga and $^{207}Pb/^{206}Pb$ ages for grains > 1.0 Ga. DZFT age peaks with 95% confidence interval were determined by Radial Plotter. The analytical details are presented in supplements Figs. S1, S2, and S3, and Table S1.

Chapter 5
Results

5.1 An Overview of the Results Section

In the Results section, researchers generally report their primary findings and make some brief comments on their findings. You may also find that in some journals, the Discussion section is merged into the Results section.

In the Results section, there are usually three common elements, namely, location element, highlighting element, and commenting element. In other words, writers are advised to let their readers know in which table or figure, what important findings can be found. Also, writers need to briefly comment on their significant findings (Cargill & Connor, 2009). Two typical case studies are as follows.

➡ *Case Study One*

Excerpt (Bakker et al., 2016)	**Comments**
3.2 Finite Element Model Results with and Without Temperature Dependency ① The calculated temperature field and resulting distributions of elastic parameters are presented in Fig. 5. ② Concentrating only on the magma storage zone, our numerical results suggest that the removal of an initially 200-m-thick ice cap reduces the pressure in the magma chamber at 5 km depth (below sea level, b.s.l.) by ~0.5 bar (see Fig. 6). ③ Pressure changes do not vary significantly between models with and without imposed layering. ④ However, this pressure change strongly depends on the depth of the magma chamber. ⑤ The pressure in a magma chamber at 1 km depth b.s.l. drops by 1.4 bar compared to 0.4 bar in a magma chamber at 10 km depth b.s.l. ⑥ The pressure decrease in the magma chamber due to ice-cap unloading varies linearly with the thickness of the ice cap. ⑦ In addition, the size of the magma chamber influences the pressure decrease slightly; for smaller magma chambers (~0.5 km radius) pressure changes are in the order of 1.0 bar compared to ~0.5 bar for large magma chamber (~5 km radius).	**Location element:** Sentence ① **Highlighting element:** Sentences ②–⑦

Chapter 5
Results

↪ Case Study Two

Excerpt (Zou et al., 2021)	Comments
4.1 Important Geochemical Features for Predicting the Crustal Thickness ① The XGBoost model is interpretable and allows to determine the importance of features during the calculation, that is, the importance of each element for predicting crustal thickness in this study. ② The importance of a feature is calculated by the average reduction of impurity, which refers to the average reduction of impurities in data when a feature is dropped. ③ As shown in Fig. 3a, the contents of all the major elements and Ba, Sr, Rb, U, and Y are the most important features used by the XGBoost model to calculate the relationship between crustal thickness and whole-rock geochemical composition. ④ In Fig. 3b, for the basalts, contents of SiO_2, Al_2O_3, TiO_2, CaO, MgO, Zr, Ba, Nb, Na_2O, K_2O, and Y are highly controlled by the crustal thickness. ⑤ Clearly, the important geochemical features of intermediate rocks and basalt are included in almost all the major elements and some trace elements.	**Advantages of the model (optional):** Sentence ① **Reviewing the method used (optional):** Sentence ② **Location element & highlighting element:** Sentences ③④ **Commenting element:** Sentence ⑤

▸ 5.2 Useful Expressions and Sentence Patterns

Useful expressions and sentence patterns used in different elements of the Results section are as follows.

A. Describing location element

* *A brief description of...**is presented in Fig. 3**.*
* *The results of...**are listed in Table 2**.*
* *...**is described in Table 4** to perform the model training process, and...**is shown in Fig. 15**.*
* *In this section, short surface temperature datasets, recorded from May to October 2019 **(see Fig. 4)**, were used to study...*
* *Spatial, monthly, and annual compositions of major ions **are illustrated in Figs. 2–4, and Table S1, respectively**, and **compared with** other world inland waters **in Table S2**.*
* *As shown in the total alkalic vs. SiO_2 diagram **(Fig. 4a)**, these rocks are mainly plotted within the fields of quartz-monzonite and syenite.*

67

B. Introducing symbols/shapes in a figure

* ***Other abbreviations are B***—*Batavia microcontinent,* ***G***—*Gulden Draak microcontinent,* ***RT***—*Rajmahal Traps...*
* ***Inset arrows show*** *vectors of relative motion between India and Australia.*
* ***Red star in (B) indicates*** *best-fit case with uniform erosion for areas below caprock.*
* ***Light blue bar shows*** *the timing of our interpreted microcontinent calving event.*
* ***Solid line indicates*** *linear regression through Young Womans Creek (YWC) data.*
* ***The numbers at the symbols represent*** *the Moho depths computed by receiver function studies.*
* ***Colored dashed lines in panel C link*** *samples from different size fractions.*
* ***Circles show*** *exact sample sites;* ***colored polygons show*** *interpreted volcanic regions...*
* ***Thick lines are*** *regression lines plotted through all individuals of a species.*
* ***These thinner lines are plotted as*** *either* ***solid*** *(statistically significant regressions, p < 0.05),* ***densely dashed*** *(p < 0.1), or* ***sparsely dashed*** *(non-significant, p > 0.1).*

C. Reporting important findings

* *Fig. 10 shows the loss function in the training process of the model with **a tendency to decrease with** increasing epochs.*
* *The slope of the transmitted waveform abruptly **decreased** after the first turning point and suddenly **increased** again after the second turning point.*
* *In the tributary rivers, the concentrations of Mg^{2+} and SO_4^{2-} **decreased gradually from** the dry season **to** the wet season.*
* *The whole YRB exhibited **a significant decreasing trend** of 0.09°C/decade, indicating greater warming in TN than in TX (Table 4).*
* *The major anions **decreased in the following order** (unit in mg/L): HCO_3^- (32.3 ± 7.5) > Cl^- (143.5 ± 24.5) > SO_4^{2-} (7.8 ± 4.9) > NO_3^- (6.1 ± 3.3) > Si (2.9 ± 1.3).*
* *The V concentration of the enclaves **decreases sharply** from 127 ppm to 68.7 ppm with increasing SiO_2 from 56.09% to 61.37%.*
* *This phenomenon results from **a reduction in** fracture stiffness...*
* *In the early stage of model training, the accuracy **rises slowly**.*
* *For the filling thickness of 2.48 mm, the transmission coefficient always **increases with** the wave amplitude in Fig. 10.*
* ***With the increase of*** *the amplitudes of the incident waves, the transmission coefficient decreases first and then increases.*
* *The filled fracture experienced strain-hardening deformation **with its** stiffness*

*monotonously **increasing in** the loading process...*

* *Excessive training will **improve the accuracy of** the train set, while it cannot provide an effective improvement in actual use in the future.*
* *At this time, the accuracy of the test set can **reach** 90.89% for the first-level classification of sedimentary, metamorphic, and igneous rocks.*
* *After **achieving a peak**, it then decreased and increased again when the PPV was larger than 5.9 m/s.*

D. Describing the relationship between two variables

* *Kumasi depicts a radial pattern from the urban core and **is associated with** a branching structure at the local scale.*
* *The radial pattern **is partly linked with** its central location in the country from which people can access other major cities in the north, south, east, and west directions.*
* *ΔTr **was positively correlated with** root water loss (Fig. 8), as expected.*
* ***There is no obvious correlation*** *that has been found between LC and the geological unit.*
* *Overall, root respiration **was significantly relative with** six of the 12 traits studied (Table 2)...*
* *We found **no apparent association between** bacteria biomass **and** bacterivores biomass.*
* *The density of Oribatidas **was not significantly related to** variables...*
* *Landslides events in layered slopes **closely depend on** the angle β between dipping direction of the slope and the dipping direction of the bedding planes.*
* *We defined a dimensionless variable χ, which **was equal to** the ratio of the fill thickness to the wavelength...*
* *It can be clearly seen that the results predicted by the static parameters of the MB-B model **matched the experimental results well**.*
* ***There is a strong linear dependency of*** *the horizontal runout on the width of the rock avalanche.*
* *In particular, water loss **was linearly related to** root area/volume ratio in all treatments except that recorded after 24 h drying...*
* *After 24 h drying, root water content **highlighted a linear and positive relation with** initial diameter (Fig. 3k).*

E. Comparing and contrasting

* *The intersection density varies from 58 per km^2 for Accra to 4 per km^2 for Ho, **whereas** the street density is from 10.8 km/km^2 for Accra to 1.2 km/km^2 for Ho.*

* Our MB-B model can characterize the above complex process well, **while** the B-B model loses the capability to do so.
* The result predicted by the MB-B model agreed very well with the experimental result. **Nevertheless**, the result predicted by the B-B model initially increased abruptly as the amplitude of the incident wave increased **but then** increased gently when the PPV of the incident wave was larger than 4.5 m/s.
* It cannot capture the effect of particle crushing on fracture stiffness. **However**, our MB-B model introduced piecewise hyperbolic functions that overcome shortcomings of the B-B model.
* **In contrast to** the above two types of thermal events, hydrothermal convection often occurs along deep fault zones.
* **On the contrary**, roots larger than 2 mm showed an evident water loss only after 5 h drying.

F. Describing data ranges

* The efficiency of the road pattern indicated by the average circuity for the districts covering the 10 regional capitals indicates similar values **ranging from** 1.046 for Accra **to** 1.104 for Sekondi-Takoradi, based on Table 2.
* The width of the Jiuqu Yihe River paleo-channel in the LGM **ranged from** 234m **to** 1,374m and the depth **ranged from** 1.3m **to** 10.1m.
* Another observation is that the dip direction of a triangle was found to **vary within the range of** at least 180° (Fig. 5, Fig. 6).

G. Showing comparative degree

* Therefore, the accuracy of batches fluctuates **more drastically than** that of epochs.
* The dispersion of northern temperate mammal body masses **is higher than** null communities and shows correlated changes with climate, consistent with resource competition and environmental filtering.
* Moreover, the worst performances for both data imputation methods correspond to October with a ΔHKNN and ΔHNN **less than** 24% and 44% respectively.
* This indicates that the uniaxial compression test can be well reproduced no matter ks **is smaller than**...
* Fig. 10 also shows that the consistence between the numerical and the experimental stress-strain curves **is much better than** that in Fig. 4.
* Indeed, after 24 h, the average strength of thin roots (40.0 ± 5.3 MPa) **was twice as large as** that in thicker roots (> 2 mm; 20.5 ± 2.6 MPa).

Chapter 5
Results

> * Comparing both data imputation methods, KNN **showed a better performance** regardless of the number of missing data.
> * For instance, drier roots **showed a much stiffer response and were more brittle**, compared with hydrated root samples (Fig. 1).

5.3 Verb Tenses in the Results Section

A. Describing location element: Simple present tense

> * Fig. 7 **represents** the contribution of purely SV particles, that is, ensembles of particles that are all in an SV remanent state.
> * The results of the bathymetry-seismic reflection correlation **are synthesized** in Fig. 3 and examples of the most characteristic bathymetric data showing morphologic expressions at the sea-bed related to fault activity **are shown** along seismic lines of the Figs. 5 and 6.

B. Introducing symbols/shapes in a figure: Simple present tense

> * Dashed contour lines **denote** negative ρ values.
> * The black dashed line **represents** the east boundary of the partially subducted oceanic lithosphere beneath the South Island.

C. Reporting the findings: Simple past tense / Simple present tense / Simple future tense

> * Particles with hard axes **aligned** closely with the applied field nucleate hard-aligned vortices at high applied field values (Fig. 8).
> * Most of the olivine grains **display** no detectable OH peaks except for some BUR samples, which have characteristic OH absorption bands at 3597, 3572, and 3525 cm^{-1} (Fig. 2c).
> * When the accuracy of the model is high, the probability of the local optimum in the solution space **will increase** significantly, so the speed of accuracy improvement **will** also **slow down** and **approach** convergence.

D. Comparing and contrasting: Simple present tense / Simple past tense / Modal auxiliaries

> * The coercivities obtained here **are considerably lower than** the commonly accepted value for natural greigites of ~60 mT.
> * For the vertical fault model, the dip angle of the triangles cutting the vertical fault

were significantly smaller than that of the model fault dip (Fig. 3).

* *However, mean field approximations can overestimate the Curie temperature, so the value of the exchange integral JAB **could be larger than** this and be consistent with experimental bounds.*

5.4 Nominalization

Nominalization is an essential feature of academic writing. It can be formed by adding affixes to verbs or adjectives. For example, by adding affixes, the verb "reduce" and the adjective "available" can be converted into the nouns "reduction" and "availability" respectively.

First, let us do a warm-up activity. Please convert the following verbs or adjectives into nouns.

assess		available	
coherent		compatible	
coordinate		dominate	
emerge		evolve	
hypothesize		intensify	
infect		justify	
modify		occupy	
occur		regulate	
refine		substitute	
subsidize		transit	

Now, look at the usages of nominalization in academic writing. For example:

* *Biologically-mediated calcification is proposed to be linked to **the saturation state of seawater**...*
* *While there is some debate regarding **the composition of the ECF** and the mechanisms that regulates it over time...*
* ***Increases in** Ω_{ECF} and pH_{ECF} shift the acid-base equilibrium in the ECF to adjust **the speciation of dissolved inorganic carbon (DIC)** to favor CO_3^{2-} over bicarbonate (HCO_3^-) ions.*

By using nominalization, your writing will be more abstract and more formal. Also, nominalization is a useful academic writing strategy because it conveys an objective, impersonal tone. Lastly, it can also make your writing more concise by packing much information into a few words.

The following example can help you to better understand the advantages of using nominalizations appropriately.

> *The plume model for microcontinent formation, where microcontinent calving is driven by plume-induced thermal weakening of continental crust, has the following characteristics.* **Firstly, it is near to a mantle plume. Secondly, it rifts from a < 25 Myr old passive continental margin. Thirdly, it is typically minor volcanism post-microcontinent formation. Lastly, it has a prolonged period of asymmetric seafloor spreading following microcontinent formation.**

The bold-faced part in the above example is not well-written, and it leaves readers with an impression that the writer is not skilled in writing. By using nominalizations, the example can be rewritten and become more formal, academic, and succinct. For example:

> *The plume model for microcontinent formation, where microcontinent calving is driven by plume-induced thermal weakening of continental crust, is characterized by: (1) proximity to a mantle plume; (2) rifting from a < 25 Myr old passive continental margin; (3) typically minor volcanism post-microcontinent formation; and (4) a prolonged period of asymmetric seafloor spreading following microcontinent formation. (Whittaker et al., 2016)*

But remember, you should be cautions when using nominalization as its overuse may make your writing obscure.

5.5 Usages of "with" in Academic Writing

The preposition "with" is widely used in academic writing. Using the preposition "with" appropriately can make your writing more cohesive, and the usages of it are as follows.

A. "with" + present participles

> * *It is an M dimensional measurement space* **with M values corresponding to** *remains poorly defined in the literature.*
> * *The Pacific-Antarctic samples are well suited to constrain how the Mo stable isotopic composition of magmas changes* **with the dominant magma differentiation processes occurring at mid-ocean ridges**.

B. "with" + past participles

* We take a visual-fitting approach to conform Indian plate motions to observed fracture zone trends in the Enderby Basin, Wharton Basin, and Perth Abyssal Plain, **with particular attention paid to** matching the curved Wharton Basin and Enderby Basin fracture zones.
* No direct observations of effective pressure at the glacier sole are available, but lake level observations were made near the proglacial lake outlet (Fig. 1) using a Hobo pressure transducer **with data logged at 15-min intervals until April 16, 2013**.

C. Noun + "with"

* H_2O contents in the coexisting cpx and opx are positively correlated and define a linear array of 2.2 **with** an excellent fit.
* The streamer had 48 seismic **traces with** inter-traces of 6.25 m and 4 hydrophones **SFH with** a spacing of 0.78 m per trace.

D. "with"-phrases

* The peridotite xenoliths derived from the Oligocene–Miocene lithospheric mantle across Zealandia, **coupled with** the very low elevation of the continent at this time, suggest little lateral variation in mantle equilibrium temperature.
* Though MT measurements **are consistent with** the presence of partial melt at mid-ocean ridges, ...
* The degree of interconnectivity can be assessed by the dihedral angle **associated with** its constituent solid-liquid phase boundaries.
* In this configuration, the melt conducts electricity **in parallel with** olivine...
* Melt pools **exist with** increasing frequency as melt fraction increases, ...
* We argue that this interpretation **is inconsistent with** microstructural observations of texturally equilibrated rocks.
* For example, hysteresis **is often observed with** identical effective pressures resulting in markedly different velocities.
* Using this setup **in combination with** Ni H-cones yielded a sensitivity of ~155 V/ppm.
* Such chemical and isotopic characteristics can, however, not **be reconciled with** mineral fractionation.
* It will be necessary to analyze samples..., ideally **in conjunction with** the analysis of mantle peridotites.

Chapter 5
Results

 **Exercises**

I. Choose the most appropriate logical connector to fill in each of the following blanks.

1. The shape of the diurnal variation is similar when the driving forces for the variation are regolith adsorption and desorption, and their coupling with the boundary layer. The adsorbed water is enriched in HDO compared to the water vapor. _____, when there is a flux from the regolith to the atmosphere, we see an increase of the near-surface D/H (i.e., the midday rise), and when there is a flux from the atmosphere to the regolith, we see a decrease of the near-surface D/H (i.e., the morning and evening drop).

    A. As a result   B. By contrast   C. Because   D. Particularly

2. The shape becomes different when condensation occurs, mainly in that the rise of D/H is delayed (see cyan line in the right panel of Fig. 5). This is _____ when the temperature of the regolith rises, water in the regolith experiences a phase change from the condensed phase to the adsorbed phase.

    A. Ø   B. if   C. because   D. so

3. The average ratio of slopes measured along topographic profiles varied from ~1 to ~2.6 (Fig. 6), _____ the average ratio of north- and south-facing mean slopes varied between ~1 and ~1.6.

    A. so   B. while   C. because   D. if

4. At high temperatures ($\geqslant 1,200°C$) and low stresses ($\leqslant 200$ MPa), strain rate is a power-law function of stress, _____ at lower temperatures and higher stresses, strain rate is an exponential function of stress.

    A. whereas   B. although   C. because   D. therefore

5. Directly above and below the magma chamber, the two models differ as much as 2 bar (Fig. 8C). _____, in temperature-independent models the pressure increases by 1 bar directly above the magma chamber, _____ in temperature-dependent models there is a pressure decrease of about 0.5 bar.

    A. For example; while   B. In addition; but
    C. Furthermore; as   D. Therefore; whereas

75

6. In addition, the fault did not experience additional shear stresses, as suggested by the lack of calcite twinning. _____, we assume this temperature is representative of the formation of the third stage of vein opening.

   A. In particular   B. Therefore   C. Furthermore   D. In addition

II. **Integrate the following simple sentences in each segment into one that is more formal and logical.**

1. Most of the Earth's surface is characterized by increases in this value. This indicates a near global increase in the intensity of the most extreme precipitation events.

   _____
   _____

2. This age is very close to a minimum seafloor age estimate of 101 ± 1 Ma from DSDP Site 256. The site is located to the north of the Batavia Knoll. But it is crucially immediately on the western side of the pseudofault. The pseudofault extends northward from the Batavia Knoll.

   _____
   _____

3. As a result, plates share an interlocking ridge-transform plate boundary. Plates also show a degree of coupling. The strength of the coupling will increase with increasing transform length. This can be achieved by requiring the breaking of older crust under shear.

   _____
   _____

4. The primary base station was also inoperable during October 2014. This leads to an increased baseline length and degraded solutions.

   _____
   _____

5. Ash B3 (93.67 ± 0.12 Ma; red star in Fig. 2a) is selected as the nominal anchor for the Iona astrochronology (RMSE = 0.121; Table 1). The same criteria noted above is used for it.

   _____
   _____

Chapter 5
Results

6. The youngest age model for the Iona core comes from the B6 ash (−0.43 Myr, Table 1). The oldest age model for the Iona core comes from the B7 ash (+0.25 Myr, Table 1).

7. Each of the ashes (with the exception of B3) is associated with three numbers. The three numbers have the same meaning as in the Libsack core, although the 2σ total uncertainty does not include stratigraphic correlation uncertainty. This is because the dated ash beds come directly from the Iona core.

8. The magnitude of carbon isotope shifts differs from the standard curve of the English Chalk. The carbon isotope shifts were observed in the Western Interior Basin (WIB) sometimes. The standard curve of the English Chalk most likely reflects local effects and different substrates (e.g., organic matter vs. carbonate).

9. This result is consistent with field observations that document rapid headward growth of low-order channels. The growth was instigated by the exposure of readily disaggregated bedrock beneath a more cohesive soil mantle.

10. Leaves from Phase 1 have relatively high SD and SI (SD = 189 ± 43 mm^{-2}, SI = 10.2 ± 1.4). Leaves from Phase 2 have relatively low SD and SI (SD = 140 ± 70 mm^{-2}, SI = 5.1 ± 0.9). Leaves from Phase 3 show a return to the high SD and SI values of Phase 1 (SD = 243 ± 67 mm^{-2}, SI = 9.9 ± 2.3) (Appendix A, Table A6).

11. At Site 1165, the ^{40}Ar/^{39}Ar thermochronological ages of minerals from pebble-sized IRD fall into two main age populations. The first one is from 487 to 571 Ma (average age 530

Ma). The other one is from 1075 to 1191 Ma (average age 1125 Ma) (Fig. 5).

12. We infer that the 450–600 Ma IRD comes from the local Prydz Bay sector and the 1075–1200 Ma IRD comes from Wilkes Land east of the Denman Glacier. This area includes the Aurora Subglacial Basin. The Basin is over 1,000 km distant from Site 1165. Our inference is based on these studies.

III. Rewrite the italicized parts in the following sentences by using nominalization appropriately.

1. Here, we focus on examining *how the relief of the westernmost Tibetan Plateau evolved* by quantifying the exhumation history of this region in the Rutog and Shiquanhe area.

2. The presence of high relief in western Tibet raises the question *whether an older, inherited relief can affect the present topography*.

3. However, *researchers analyzed detrital zircons contained in the red beds further north in the Domar area and their analysis indirectly suggests* a Jurassic deposition age.

4. *We further study the work by Kramers et al. (2013)* on a very unusual diamond-rich rock fragment found in the area of southwest Egypt in the southwestern side of the Libyan Desert Glass strewn field.

5. Nevertheless, in each scenario, *we should know the movement of mid-depth water between 2,000 and 3,000 m, likely Pacific Deep Water (PDW).*

6. In addition to the Xe–Q composition, *we observe radiogenic ^{129}Xe (from the decay of short-lived radioactive ^{129}I) is excessive.*

7. Our study does not confirm *there are exotic noble gases* (e.g., G component) that led Kramers et al. (2013) to propose that Hypatia is a remnant of a comet nucleus that impacted the Earth.

8. *The fact that this area does not have graphite-bearing target rock* further supports the conclusions that Hypatia must be extraterrestrial.

9. *Comparing any related predictions* with the seismic structure of the deep mantle *is necessary, as it will improve* our understanding of the Earth's long-term evolution.

10. *We use the digital rock physics approach to determine* the bulk electrical conductivity of partially molten rocks, *which can have* fine control on the physics and material properties of the system.

11. In this work we extend the study by Kramers et al. (2013). *We conduct the isotopic analyses of all five noble gases in several Mg-sized fragments of Hypatia in two different laboratories (CRPG Nancy, France and ETH Zürich, Switzerland). We conduct a nitrogen isotope investigation performed both at CRPG (Nancy) and IPG-Paris.*

_____

_____

12. *They attempted to determine the oxygen isotopic composition in Hypatia by the Nancy Cameca 1280 ion probe, but they failed because the size of oxygen-bearing phases reduced and because there were contaminants and important amounts of water.*

_____

_____

Chapter 6
Discussions

6.1 An Overview of the Discussion Section

In research papers, the Discussion section usually follows the Results section. In this section, writers can review their important findings, discuss reasons contributing to the findings, make comparisons between their present findings and previous ones, introduce unexpected results, and offer suggestions for future studies (Cargill & Connor, 2009). Three typical case studies are as follows.

▶ Case Study One

Excerpt (Ma et al., 2019)	Comments
5.3 Comparison with Other Geological Records That Express Secular Resonances ① Fig. 6 summarizes the geological records that report the cycles of s4–s3 and g4–g3 from the present to 270 Ma. ② Note that s4–s3 is less often reported than g4–g3. ③ During the interval from 50–100 Ma, when a possible transition of secular resonances took place according to the theoretical solutions, previous studies suggest that the 2.4-Myr g4–g3 cycle exists in most of the interval (50–80 Ma). ④ Our new study, covering 82–97 Ma, demonstrates the 2.4-Myr cycle and its temporary switch from 2.4 Myr to 1.2 Myr in g4–g3, and also reveals a 1.2-Myr cycle in s4–s3 that occurs throughout much of the study interval.	**Summarizing the findings of the present study:** Sentence ① **Making a comparison between previous studies and present studies:** Sentences ②–④

▶ Case Study Two

Excerpt (Carmichael et al., 2018)	Comments
4.3 How Well Does HadCM3L Represent Extremes? ① In Fig. 8, two observational metrics for extreme precipitation- the maximum annual 1 day precipitation rate (Rx1) and the contribution to MAP of days above the 99th percentile rate (R99p) are compared with the preindustrial 1 × CO_2 HadCM3L simulation.	**Summarizing the findings of the present study and explaining the implications of the findings:** Sentences ①–⑤

Chapter 6
Discussions

(Continued)

Excerpt (Carmichael et al., 2018)	Comments
② In both cases, the spatial variation in the indices suggest that the model performs relatively well at simulating relative differences across the Earth's surface. ③ However, the model does a much poorer job in the simulation of the absolute precipitation rates associated with the extreme "tail" of the distribution. ④ Maximum model-simulated values are typically around a third of the observational values. ⑤ Therefore, percentage change plots or qualitative interpretations (e.g., Figs. 2, 3) may be more robust than absolute rates (e.g., Fig. 4).	
⑥ Two main groups of reasons may explain why the model underestimates the magnitude of absolute extreme precipitation rates: (1) grid resolution and (2) model parameterizations. ⑦ In the case of the former, different methods for comparing pointwise (station, gauge) estimates of extreme precipitation to those resolved on a coarse model grid remain largely untested. ⑧ By their very nature, extreme events are very localized and discontinuous. ⑨ Although the HadEx2 dataset is based on ~11,300 precipitation gauge data which are interpolated to a regular grid, whether these data are truly comparable to model data is highly uncertain; Chen & Knutson (2008) found that differences of up to 30% in daily averaged extreme precipitation rates occurred over the United States, according to interpolation scheme and whether GCM precipitation was considered to represent a point estimate or areal average rate. ⑩ Furthermore, dynamical features associated with extremes (e.g., storm tracks) are in general better represented in high resolution models than in low resolution models.	**Explaining why the model undervalues the magnitude of absolute extreme precipitation rates:** Sentences ⑥–⑩

↪ Case Study Three

Excerpt (Bakker et al., 2016)	Comments
4.2 Broader Implications of Temperature-dependent Elastic Properties in Time-independent Models ① The effect at depth caused by a reduction of the vertical load due to ice-sheet removal has not been quantified before using temperature-	**The gap in previous studies and the necessity to address the gap:** Sentences ①②

(Continued)

Excerpt (Bakker et al., 2016)	Comments
dependent elastic parameters. ② The large difference between temperature-dependent and temperature-independent models shows that assuming temperature-independent elastic properties for the host rock does not accurately represent the physical state of shallow magmatic systems, and should be reconsidered. ③ In low-temperature domains (shallow and/or at significant distance to the magma chamber), the pressure changes in the basement and in the edifice observed in this study (i.e., temperature-dependent) are comparable with previous findings (temperature-independent). ④ We ascribe this to the relatively low temperatures in the brittle domain away from the magmatic reservoir, so that constant elastic properties are an adequate assumption. ⑤ However, significant differences occur in close proximity to the magma chamber and at depth and close to the brittle–ductile transition. ⑥ There, temperature-independent elastic properties are a poor assumption when modeling volcanic environments and regions are close to the solidus in a time-independent manner. ⑦ In most previous studies, magma chambers are represented as a circle (sphere) or ellipse (ellipsoid), yet in nature the magma chamber is likely more complex. ⑧ In our models, we also prescribe the magma chamber as an ellipse at depth, but it is only associated with a temperature boundary in the temperature-dependent models.	**Reporting one of the study findings and discussing the reason contributing to it:** Sentences ③④ **Reporting unexpected findings:** Sentences ⑤⑥ **Making a comparison between previous studies and present studies:** Sentences ⑦⑧

6.2 Useful Expressions and Sentence Patterns

Useful expressions and sentence patterns used in different elements of the Discussion section are as follows.

A. Introducing similarities and differences

* Our data **are thus in good agreement with** this previous interpretation.
* This estimate **is in accordance with** inferred Miocene paleoelevation of 1.0–2.4 km for the basin and surrounding areas determined from paleobotanical data.
* Tensile strength of Ulex europaeus **was also close to** that reported for similar species belonging to the Fabaceae family such as Spartium Junceum.

Chapter 6
Discussions

* *This **is supported by** S-isotope compositions for the shergottites considered in this study, which do not show any anomalous D33S.*
* *Our data from the Xiaolongtan Basin, **however, are inconsistent with** previous geomorphic studies by...*
* *However, our inferred timing of crustal flow (13 Ma) in SE Yunnan **is not compatible with**...*
* ***In contrast to** the above ground fungal communities, we have limited understanding of...*

B. Explaining causality

* *Uplift of SE Yunnan **is probably the consequence of** lower crustal flow beneath the plateau margin since at least the Early Miocene.*
* *Assuming crustal flow **was singularly responsible for** the elevation of the region, constant near-modern elevations of NW Yunnan.*
* ***It is therefore possible that** the presence of a weak, ..., initiated the uplift of the northeastern Qiangtang Block in the Middle Eocene.*
* *This base level fall **may be triggered by** the activity of the Xianshuihe fault since ~13 Ma and the reactivation of the Longmen Shan fault since ~12–8 Ma.*
* *In this region, the ionization **is due to** the photoionization process of nitric oxide (NO) by Hydrogen Lyman series-alpha radiation (wavelength 121.5 nanometer) during daytime.*
* *Wu et al. (2011) **attribute** their elevated Fe at shallower depths **to** a dispersal of Fe from the Loihi seamount located approximately 2,000 km to the north.*
* *This dispersal **might be the cause of** the higher concentrations of Fe over a wider range of depths.*
* *We **ascribe** this negative effect **to** the higher probability for raindrops to split up at branches.*
* *Given these arguments on melt focusing into the arc crust, **it is unlikely that** source-related variations in melt chemistry (hypothesis ii) can be preserved.*
* *Influenced by the tectonic thermal events that **were caused by** the enhancement of tectonic compression and magmatic activity in the deep lithosphere...*
* *Contamination of mantle-derived magma with such rocks would **have resulted in** lower $\delta^{18}O$ and lower $\epsilon Hf(t)$ in the contaminated magma.*
* *Given the structural and morphological observations outlined above, we **propose that** surface uplift of SE Yunnan **may be the result of** lower crustal flow in this area since at least ~13 Ma.*

C. Showing implications of the study findings

* ***These observations together suggest that*** *deposition of Eocene strata and their near-modern elevation in NW Yunnan at ~40 Ma were not related to...*
* ***Our findings propose that*** *independent self-sustaining human-to-human spread is already present in multiple major Chinese cities.*
* ***This implies that*** *the Tibetan hinterland may have exhibited a thickened crust by ~60–50 Ma.*
* ***This discrepancy infers that*** *this region has a 150 K higher temperature than the normal geotherm because of the presence of a hot plume beneath Hawaii.*
* *They **may be helpful to better understand** the mechanism of the dynamic triggering of earthquakes.*
* *In addition, this transect **fills a gap in** the sediment record likely due to poor foraminiferal preservation (Fig. 3).*
* ***It is therefore key that*** *depth habitat, seasonality, and ecology are regionally resolved for this species.*
* *Therefore, **the present study may provide insights into the effects of** soil moisture on...*
* *More broadly, **our experimental results indicate that** mantle potential temperatures along all ocean spreading centers are hotter than existing estimates.*
* ***This study proves that*** *the electrical conductivity of olivine aggregate shows a strong water-content dependence.*
* ***Our experimental measurements demonstrate that*** *the development of an interconnected network...*
* *In this study, both two and three-dimensional liquid distributions **reveal that** silicate melt is dominated by tubular melt channels.*
* *With increasing temperature, the increasing frequency of N = 3 and 4 and the decreasing silicate melt-mineral dihedral angle **are both indicative of** the increasing melt connectivity and permeability.*
* ***Field observations indicate that*** *the resulting contrast in downslope soil transport efficiency is a consequence of coarse sediment derived from the caprock.*

D. Reporting limitations of the present study

* *However, these efforts have been **limited by a lack of** ground shaking data for many of the events in the database.*
* ***One problem for*** *identifying the maximum fill of a channel **was lack of** preservation of the section and erosion by subsequent channeling.*
* *Nonetheless, our study **has several major limitations**.*
* *Although we see no evidence for such complications at Young Womans Creek, **it is***

not clear whether such signals are expected or resolvable.

* ***It should be noted that the experimental study ignored the effect of*** *the triaxial stress state.*
* ***Uncertainties, however, remain*** *about the deglaciation history of the Lake District. Earliest signs of deglaciation are dated to 24.8–28.0 kyr...**Nevertheless**, the timeframe of deglaciation for some of the lakes coincides with the decline of turbidite deposition along similar latitudes.*
* ***Finally, we should point out that we are uncertain if****..., **but such uncertainty can be addressed by analyzing**...*

E. Reporting unexpected findings

* *However, the results of the present study is considerably lower than those (1.6–2.9 GPa) determined at 23 GPa, 1,800 K...**One of the causes for the discrepancy may be** complexity of the deformation geometry of the RDA experiments, as discussed later.*
* ***Thus, it might be expected that*** *hillslope form reveals a similar contrast.* ***Instead, we find that*** *hillslopes where the caprock has been preserved on ridges are systematically steeper (mean slope = 20°–30°; Fig. 2B) than hillslopes...**We hypothesize that this contrast in hillslope erodibility emerges due to**...*

F. Offering suggestions for future studies

* *In future studies, it would be of interest to test...*
* *Future works will mainly focus on...*
* *The effects of interparticle magnetostatic...**are left for a future study**.*
* *This provides additional evidence to support the pattern of the La2004 model in this time interval, and **can be further investigated to evaluate**...*
* ***Further studies are therefore needed to investigate*** *the influence of these factors.*
* ***Therefore,*** *...**should be used to more accurately determine** the homogenization temperatures of the coexisting inclusion assemblages.*
* *Further experimental studies may provide...*
* *But whether...**remains for further study**.*
* ***A further study*** *of these locations **may enable further unraveling of** how plumes and tectonic processes interact to break continents apart.*

6.3 Verb Tenses in the Discussion Section

A. Introducing similarities and differences: Simple present tense

* *The ages proposed for these horizons **are consistent with** the interpretations of Franke et al. (2015).*
* *Di Muro et al. (2014) stress that the high-temperature range (> 1200°C) **is inconsistent with** the low average Fo content in olivine and the relatively evolved composition of aphyric lavas and glassy matrix melts.*

B. Explaining causality: Simple present tense / Modal auxiliaries

* *These different trends **are possibly controlled by** inherited fracture zones within the oceanic lithosphere...*
* *In this scenario, dykes that do not intercept previously emplaced magma pockets **may result in** failed eruptions.*

C. Showing implications of the present study: Simple present tense / Simple past tense / Modal auxiliaries

* *Our study **suggests** that the response time of a system is significantly influenced by temporal changes of connectivity.*
* *However, our results **have** qualitative applicability beyond greigites, for magnetic minerals with cubic MCA such as magnetite and iron, which are known to occur as non-interacting particles.*
* *However, turbidites do not mirror a sedimentary signal that shows increased Qs due to glacial melting, suggesting that sediment **was released into** partly ice-free piedmont lakes.*
* *These findings **provided** a novel mechanism of tripartite interactions between the devastating fungal pathogen, ...*
* *Electrical conductivity profiles **can provide constraints on** the thermal and chemical states of the mantle.*

D. Reporting limitations / unexpected findings: Simple present tense / Simple past tense / Modal auxiliaries

* *Although the spatial patterns described here are specific to Eocene boundary*

Chapter 6
Discussions

> *conditions, **it is noteworthy that there are several similarities** between simulated PETM behavior and future predicted precipitation change.*
>
> * ***Their study also demonstrates that** the occurrence of the rarest events can differ markedly from other measures of the distribution.*
>
> * *In addition, the effect of loading rate on the compression behavior of the filled fracture **was not considered in the study of** the seismic response of the filled fracture.*
>
> * *However, these nucleation and annihilation events **make a negligible contribution to** the FORC diagram because the change in magnetization of a particle nucleating/annihilating a hard-aligned vortex from/to a SD state **can be** as low as 1%.*

E. Offering suggestions for future studies: Simple present tense / Simple future tense / Modal auxiliaries

> * ***More studies that contrast** the depths and magmatic processes inferred from monitoring networks with those obtained from crystals and host melt inclusions **should be able to** clarify the different architecture of volcanic systems.*
>
> * *In the future, larger datasets **will enable**...*
>
> * *However, the role of magma supply rates that we propose to shape the plumbing systems of these volcanoes **should be further investigated by** numerical or analogue experiments.*
>
> * ***Further work on** the triple sulfur isotope composition of pyrite and H2S in modern SD-AOM-dominated environments **is needed** before we can apply these new findings to the sedimentary record.*
>
> * ***Further comparisons** of metrics utilized for future climate studies with paleoclimate simulations **could assist in** identifying changes that are common to warm climate periods.*

6.4 Using Hedges

Hedges can be used to express tentativeness and possibility in communication (Hyland, 1996). It is necessary for writers to acquire how to use hedges appropriately, as they are an important feature of scientific writing. Different kinds of hedges and their examples in geoscience papers are shown below.

A. Modal auxiliaries

> * *However, it indicates a more local effect **should** be considered.*
>
> * *Rapid local ice loss during this period, which has been linked to reverse bed slopes in*

the Amery Depression, **would** result in rapid land uplift and a fall in the height of the geoid, both of which would offset the far-field eustatic signal.
* However, there is no evidence for a significant regional event that **can** be correlated with the main exhumation event at about 10–9 Ma.
* Because the confidence envelopes overlap, the discrepancy between these four models **could** be due to insufficient resolution of our data.
* Second, western Tibet exhumation **may** be related to regional geodynamics.
* A similar process **might** have also led to the super-chondritic Si/Mg ratio in H chondrites, and even to that in all OC.
* Our models suggest that these processes **may not** be affected as dramatically as currently thought.

B. Verbs

* We **assume** that the first stage of mode I vein opening corresponds to the first increment of the Cotiella thrust fault activity.
* Furthermore, the Shiquanhe thrust **seems to** have a limited lateral extent (≤ 100 km) and its throw is about 7 km.
* The samples **appear to** record different rates of rapid cooling...

C. Adjectives

* Another **possible** explanation of the ~11–9 Ma event is the reorganization of the river network.
* In summary, the most **likely** scenario is that during a first stage, the Bangong valley was connected to the sea and deep valleys formed (Fig. 8A).

D. Adverbs

* Our reconstruction is **basically** in line with other estimates of continental temperatures.
* Moreover, the continental temperature patterns inferred from palaeobotanical data **largely** agree with results obtained from coeval marine archives.
* This area of the Natal valley is **possibly** associated with volcanic seamounts which might be related to the EARS extension tectonics.
* This difference is **partially** reflected in the small but statistically insignificant decrease in $\delta^{11}BSK$ and $\delta^{13}CSK$ values.
* Therefore, some of the faults were **probably** already active as soon as Miocene times which is consistent with the tectonic framework of the EARS.
* These faults are **mostly** straight (planar), whereas the main faults are **mainly** listric north of 20°S.

Chapter 6
Discussions

E. Other expressions

* In this model, **it is assumed that** all fluids contribute evenly across all species.
* **It is reasonable to assume that** the Mg content of whiteschist is largely derived from metasomatic fluids due to the low Mg content of metagranite.
* **It may be that** some fluids contribute more of one species and less of another (i.e., the contribution of a fluid to the total gas budget is not equal to the equilibrium composition).
* **It would be possible**, given pyrrhotite compositions and modal abundances for each magma type, **to** calculate the loss of S to the solid phase.
* **It seems unlikely that** this is related to the unusually high salinity levels (> 40) seen in the Gulf of Aqaba (Eilat).
* As such **it is probable that** $CaCO_3$ analyzed from these tows experienced irradiation levels well above those required to compensate for the acidifying effects of respired CO_2.

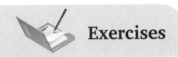

Exercises

I. Read the following paragraph and find out the four errors contained in the underlined sentences. Each underlined sentence contains only one error. In each case, only one word is involved. You should proofread the sentences and correct the errors.

As briefly summarized in the introduction, **1.** <u>the most recent seismic tomographic study has supported the model of a mantle flow induce by an edge effect in the mantle circulation</u> at the lithospheric step between the thick East Antarctic Craton and thin Ross Sea crust based on structural and morphotectonic analyses, aeromagnetic data, and thermobarometry with mantle xenoliths. The edge flow model is also strongly consistent with the E–W fast directions from the seismic anisotropic results. Based on the edge flow model and our tomographic results, we tried to explain the origin of the low-velocity anomalies beneath Mt. Melbourne and the Priestley Fault. **2.** <u>In order to infer the shapes of the anomalies from our inversion results, we should consider the spatial distributions of the resolution in addition to the underestimate amplitudes of the anomalies</u>. A resolution test was performed with the same input model in Fig. 3 except for L2 coming vertically from a 120 km depth and no dipping to the eastern side of the model; the recovered model was very similar to our best target model, as shown in Fig. 4. The resolution tests revealed limited resolutions for the structure at the eastern edge of the model space and small structures over the entire model space, and we cannot rule out that the anomaly beneath Mt. Melbourne came from deeper depths on the eastern side. Our model showed no low-velocity anomalies below a depth of 120 km, and the low-velocity anomaly beneath the Priestley Fault rose to shallower depths up to ~30 km. **3.** <u>One possible mechanism is that the edge-driven convection due to different thicknesses of the lithosphere cause mantle partial melting localized just beneath Mt. Melbourne or the eastern side at a depth of ~110 km.</u> **4.** <u>The partially melted material moves up to a depth of 40 km beneath Mt. Melbourne and stretches simultaneously to the southern tip of the Deep Freeze Range at depths of 40–80 km, which the Moho depths are relatively shallow.</u> (Park et al., 2015)

II. Rewrite the italicized parts in the following sentences by using appropriate hedging expressions.

1. The continuity of the diatomite is episodically interrupted by turbidites rich in plant material, *which represent lakeside slumping*.

_____

_____

Chapter 6
Discussions

2. *We confirm* that rain-induced speed-up events *have a positive contribution to* displacement of between 2% and 13% per annum.

3. At first glance, *these results conflict with our interpretation* that fossil leaves in the Foulden Maar sediments record changes in Ca. However, the anthropogenic Ca rise of the recent past does not provide a good analogy to the Foulden Maar record, due to differences in timescale.

4. In any case, because our samples are located ⩾ 140 km east of the proposed Angmong fault, and would be in the hanging wall, *this fault will never affect their exhumation history.*

5. *Our findings must have important implications* for future numerical studies and the understanding of various geological processes.

6. *Such pressure change must cause* deglaciation-triggered melt pumping from the mantle, which in turn *replenishes* the shallow magmatic reservoirs.

7. *This is related to* the rheological properties of these levels which can correspond to relatively plastic clays-rich horizons.

93

8. *It must be the fact that* the 2017 discharge measurements do not reflect longer-term conditions.

   _____

   _____

9. The crystal-rich magma would have encountered a preexisting structural discontinuity, *definitely compensating* for the lack of buoyancy due to the high crystal cargo and triggering a lateral eruption.

   _____

   _____

   _____

10. During the LGM and the deglacial, *turbidity currents must be triggered by* various mechanisms (earthquakes, storms, hyperpycnal discharge, submarine slope failure), which we are unable to resolve.

    _____

    _____

11. Compared to Site A and H, Site SA features only a single offshore record *that is unrepresentative for* the entire region as absolute values of turbidite frequency and thickness strongly depend on site location.

    _____

    _____

    _____

12. This area of the Natal valley *is associated with* volcanic seamounts *which is related to* the EARS extension tectonics.

    _____

    _____

Chapter 6
Discussions

III. There are four blanks in each paragraph below, only one of which needs to be filled in with a missing sentence. Fit the following three sentences into the best positions.

A. *This scenario is supported by two sets of independent evidence.*

1. _____ The absence of Middle Jurassic–Cretaceous marine sediments within the Songpan–Ganzi, Kunlun, and northern Tianshuihai terranes suggests that large parts of northwestern Tibet formed positive topography above sea level at this time (Fig. 8B). **2.** _____ First, thick Jurassic–Cretaceous terrestrial deposits in the piedmont of the eastern Pamir were apparently sourced from a Permian–Triassic arc-accretionary prism equivalent to the Songpan–Ganzi and Kunlun terranes. **3.** _____ Second, a growing body of evidence shows significant crustal shortening and thickening throughout western Tibet and the Pamir during the Middle–Late Mesozoic, probably related to the Lhasa–Qiangtang collision, or alternatively protracted underthrusting of the Lhasa terrane beneath the Qiangtang. **4.** _____ (Cao, 2015)

B. *Furthermore, the proposed geometry of the SSCF (whether north- or south-dipping) is unknown, and the age, surface expression, subsurface-dip, activity, and slip rate have not been thoroughly investigated.*

Previous geological mapping has included minor unnamed fault segments along a section of the proposed SSCF with no indication of the subsurface geometry or connectivity. **5.** _____ Additionally, a structure named the Pagenkopp fault has been mapped from well data at the eastern end of the proposed surface trace of the SSCF. **6.** _____ However, despite much previous mapping within the Santa Clara River Valley (Fig. 1), a continuous fault along the northern Santa Clara River Valley has not been characterized by any geological or geomorphic field evidence, or subsurface data. **7.** _____ Without accurate characterization of the SSCF, a rigorous assessment of seismic hazard in this densely populated and tectonically active area of southern California remains incomplete. **8.** _____ (Hughes et al., 2018)

C. *However, it apparently fails to explain Late Oligocene–Early Miocene brittle upper crustal deformation and rock uplift along the West Kunlun mountain front.*

Two end-member models have been proposed to account for Neogene tectonics and magmatism in the West Kunlun ranges. In a northward wedging model, the West Kunlun orogen behaves like a wedge overriding the Tarim plate via thrusting along the frontal faults, and the Tarim lithosphere plunges southward deeply beneath the mountains as imaged by teleseismic data. **9.** _____ This model explains the upper crustal deformation pattern and deep lithosphere architecture of northwestern Tibet, but fails to explain Neogene magmatism in the Tianshuihai and Karakoram. 10. _____ The second model of lower crustal flow predicts the existence of partially molten zones in the middle to lower crust beneath the Tibetan Plateau. 11. _____ This model is used to explain the Late Miocene–Quaternary eruption of shoshonitic volcanic rocks in northwestern Tibet. 12. _____ (Cao, 2015)

IV. In the following paragraphs, some sentences are missing. Fill in the blanks with the most suitable ones from the list A–E. There is one extra choice, which does not fit in any of the gaps.

5.4.3 Paleocene–Early Eocene

Paleocene–Early Eocene magmatism in the Tianshuihai terrane, synchronous with volcanism in the Qiangtang terrane of central Tibet, favors a model of partial melting of a thickened lower crust, consistent with geophysical observations of a high-conductivity, low-velocity zone in the lower to middle crust across western Tibet. Similar crustal thickening and melting are also inferred from dehydration melting along with prograde metamorphism of hydrous silicate glass inclusions in xenoliths from the deep crust of the southeastern Pamir. However, the magnitude of crustal deformation seems insufficient to induce considerable regional surface uplift, compared with that in the Middle–Late Mesozoic.

1. _____ Scattered Paleocene–Early Eocene peak ages with large lag-time intervals indicate that the south Kunlun probably remained in the partial annealing zone at this time, and was exhumed to the surface and eroded immediately to the foreland basin by the Late Oligocene–Miocene (see Section 5.4.4 for discussion). In principle, when a crustal column is exhumed, cooling ages of rocks young downward along the structural section, successively presenting unreset, partially reset, and younger fully reset ages. 2. _____ Accordingly, static Early Cretaceous (P3), moving Paleocene–Early Eocene (P2), and moving Late Oligocene–Miocene (P1) peak ages, derived from a common source in the south Kunlun likely record an age pattern as predicted from a structurally exhumed section (Fig. 6).

3. _____ Third, a growing body of evidence shows that a more extensive phase of surface uplift and rock exhumation occurred later, during Neogene times. 4. _____ The Main Pamir–Tam Karaul thrust system could have served as a first-order tectonic boundary defining the northwest limit of Late Mesozoic to Eocene Tibet, as tentatively outlined in previous studies. (Cao, 2015)

Chapter 6
Discussions

A. Second, the persistence of the Paratethys Sea in the southern Tarim basin implies that the north Kunlun terrane resided near sea level during the Early Eocene.

B. We thus infer that the Early Cenozoic crustal architecture of northwestern Tibet was largely inherited from pre-existing thickened crust, consistent with geological observations in the nearby Domar area in western Qiangtang.

C. First, we see little evidence for prominent rock exhumation in the study area during the Early Cenozoic, although thrusting-driven erosional exhumation, related to the India–Asia collision, probably occurred at ~50 Ma in the northeastern Pamir.

D. Any valid geodynamic mechanism should explain the first-order pattern of tectonism, magmatism, and exhumation that approximately commenced during Late Oligocene–Early Miocene times across western Tibet.

E. This age pattern can be imprinted on detrital samples collected in the foreland basin.

Chapter 7
Conclusions and Acknowledgements

7.1 An Overview of the Conclusions Section

In the Conclusions section, usually the last part of the main body of a research paper, writers need to summarize their study methods and findings, reiterate their study significance and contributions, and give suggestions for future research. Some readers may think that the Conclusions section is similar to the Abstract section, as the components of them are similar, and both should be short. However, there are differences between these two sections in summarization level and function. The summarization level of the Abstract section is higher than that of the Conclusions section. In addition, the Abstract section leaves readers with an impression of being general and intriguing, and serves as a function of attracting readers' attention, while the Conclusions section aims to summarize research findings and emphasize research significance. It is inevitable that the Abstract and Conclusion sections may contain the same information. In this case, writers should express the same information in the two sections by using different words and expressions.

In the following contrast between the Conclusions section and the Abstract section, both of them analyze the reason contributing to the first pulse of rapid exhumation, but the writers use different words and expressions to explain it.

- **Abstract:** *The first cooling event, at about 20 Ma,* ① *was likely related to* ② *a major geodynamic event such as slab breakoff that induced contemporaneous potassic and ultrapotassic magmatism. The second rapid cooling pulse from ~11 Ma to 9 Ma and subsequent negligible cooling was most likely controlled by a local factor such as Indus and Shyok river network reorganization* ③ *caused by dextral motion of the Karakorum fault. We discuss these interpretations and their limitations in this contribution… (Gourbet et al., 2016)*
- **Conclusions:** *We* ① *attribute the first pulse of rapid exhumation to the* ② *geodynamic processes responsible for the early Miocene potassic and ultrapotassic volcanic activity occurring in this region. The latest pulse is related to a river network reorganization* ③ *due to the strike-slip motion of the Karakorum fault that connected the Bangong valley to the paleo-Shyok river, leading to an externally drained system and a transient acceleration of the erosion… (Gourbet et al., 2016)*

After making a contrast between the two sections, two typical case studies are given below, through which the elements that should be included in the Conclusions section are shown.

Chapter 7
Conclusions and Acknowledgements

➤ Case Study One

Excerpt (Gourbet et al., 2016)	Comments
① Apatite (U–Th–Sm)/He and ^{4}He/^{3}He thermochronometry in the Rutog area (Rutog batholith), between the Karakorum dextral strike-slip fault and the sinistral Longmu–Gozha Co strike-slip fault, indicate that western Tibet experienced slow exhumation rates since the Oligocene, except during two moderate exhumation pulses occurring from 19 Ma to 17 Ma and ~ 11–9 Ma, leading to a total incision of about 1,500 m. ② We attribute the first pulse of rapid exhumation to the geodynamic processes responsible for the early Miocene potassic and ultrapotassic volcanic activity occurring in this region. ③ The latest pulse is related to a river network reorganization due to the strike-slip motion of the Karakorum fault that connected the Bangong valley to the paleo-Shyok river, leading to an externally drained system and a transient acceleration of the erosion. ④ The exhumation has been negligible since 9 Ma, partly because western Tibet has been mostly internally drained since 4 Ma, due to the damming of the Bangong Lake. ⑤ Finally, this case study shows the importance of river network distribution on the control of exhumation. ⑥ Not only does the river distribution control whether or not geodynamic change can be imprinted on the thermochronological record, but it can also directly affect the exhumation rate.	**Reviewing primary findings:** Sentence ① **Discussing results briefly:** Sentences ②–④ **Emphasizing study significance:** Sentences ⑤⑥

➤ Case Study Two

Excerpt (Pierce et al., 2017)	Comments
① The delivery of large pulses of ice-rafted material from 14.1 Ma to 13.8 Ma found at IODP Site U1356 and ODP Site 1165 provides a direct and proximal record of the mid-Miocene Climate Transition (MMCT) that links the discontinuous evidence for this major climate transition from terrestrial Antarctic sites to far-field oxygen isotope and sea level records. ② A series of MMCT IRD pulses at Site U1356 suggest that the transition includes stepped advance and retreat of the ice edge superimposed on the overall MMCT ice advance. ③ Provenance	**Reviewing primary findings:** Sentences ①③

Excerpt (Pierce et al., 2017)	Comments
results using $^{40}Ar/^{39}Ar$ of ice-rafted hornblende grains from the MMCT at Site U1356 show that: (1) The MMCT IRD is dominated by thermochronological ages of 1,400–1,550 Ma, the same age as the Mertz Shear Zone and the eastern side of the Adélie and Gawler Cratons, but in contrast to the majority of recent IRD from core tops along this sector of the coast, which has a make-up more similar to the coastal outcrops. ④ This implies that the edge of the MMCT ice sheet was eroding bedrock sources inland from the present-day ice edge. (2) ⑤ The IRD data are strong evidence for the presence of a 1,400–1,550 Ma thermochronological province running along the eastern edge of the Adélie Craton, which would geographically link the eastern Gawler Craton of Australia and the area inland of the Nimrod Glacier in the Transantarctic Mountains, forming the continuous eastern margin of the Mawson Continent. (3) ⑥ The $^{40}Ar/^{39}Ar$ signature also points to active erosion of the deep upper troughs of the Western Basin, which include the Mertz Shear Zone and the eastern Adélie Craton, by paleo ice streams during the MMCT. ⑦ The changing provenance of fine-grained sediment over the MMCT, based on Nd isotope data, implies repeated advance of the ice sheet from the Antarctic interior into the Wilkes Subglacial Basin (WSB). ⑧ The Nd data also suggest that the jökulhlaups previously inferred from bedrock topography in the Central Basin of the Wilkes Subglacial Basin could have occurred during the MMCT. … ⑨ This work highlights the value of provenance studies and of scientific offshore drilling for revealing the history of the Antarctic ice sheets and the geology hidden under the ice.	**Discussing results briefly:** Sentences ②, ④–⑧ **Emphasizing study significance:** Sentence ⑨

7.2 An Overview of the Acknowledgements Section

It is very necessary for writers to thank the researchers who offered assistance and the organizations that financially supported their research at the end of their research paper. Two typical case studies are shown below.

Chapter 7
Conclusions and Acknowledgements

➦ Case Study Three

Excerpt (Pierce et al., 2017)	Comments
Acknowledgements This work was funded by NSF Grant ANT 0944489 to TW, TvdF, and SRH; NSF Grant ANT 538580 to SRH, TvdF, and SLG; NSF Grant ANT 0838842 to SP; Royal Society Grant IE110878 to SRH and TvdF, and NERC funding to TvdF (NE/L004607/1, NE/I006257/1, NE/H014144/1, NE/H025162/1). ELP thanks G. Mesko, J. Gombiner, and K. Kreissig for lab assistance. We thank IODP for the Site U1356 and Site 1165 core samples.	The writers express their sincere gratitude to the institutions that financially supported their study and the researchers who gave them pertinent and inspiring suggestions and assisted their study.

➦ Case Study Four

Excerpt (Gourbet et al., 2016)	Comments
Acknowledgements We thank Kerry Gallagher for his help with QTQt and Nick Fylstra for his assistance in the Noble Gas Thermochronometry lab. Liu Xiaobing and Liu Xiaohan are acknowledged for their assistance for organizing fieldwork, François Senebier for his technical assistance at ISTerre (Grenoble), and Nicolas Arnaud for helping us with the Ar data. M. Murphy and an anonymous reviewer helped improving this manuscript. This study was supported by the Explo'ra Doc program of the Région Rhône-Alpes, the SYSTER (INSU) and the Cai Yuanpei No. 531 27968UC (French Ministry of Foreign Affairs) programs.	The writers express their sincere gratitude to the institutions that financially supported their study and the researchers who gave them pertinent and inspiring suggestions and assisted their study.

7.3 Useful Expressions and Sentence Patterns

Useful expressions and sentence patterns for showing gratitude are as follows.

* ***This study was funded by*** *the Geological Survey of China (No: 1212011121261).*
* ***This study was supported by*** *a Victoria University of Wellington Research Establishment Grant.*
* ***This work was aided by*** *NERC Ph.D. studentships.*
* ***This manuscript has also benefited greatly from*** *the thoughtful comments of reviewers Alain Burgisser and Andrea Di Muro.*

- ***We thank** P. Gillette and T. Capo **for** providing us with space in the University of Miami's experimental hatchery facility to conduct these experiments.*
- ***We are indebted to** Gavin Foster, Carrie Lear, Dan Murphy, Fred Le Moigne, Helen Griffin, and Anya Crocker **for** their advice and helpful discussions of the manuscript.*
- ***We wish to thank** Alpha Exploration Ltd. **for** providing data for this study, and especially to Alasdair Smith for his support.*
- ***The authors are grateful to** the anonymous reviewers and the editor **for** their helpful and constructive comments that greatly helped improve the manuscript.*
- *Wei Huang, Andy Juhl, Betina Fleming, and Nicole deRoberts **are acknowledged for** technical support.*
- *Joseph Knight **kindly provided insightful discussions and reviews** which improved the paper.*

7.4 Sentence Structures

Simple sentences, complex sentences, and compound sentences are widely used in academic writing.

A simple sentence is a sentence with only one independent clause. Though a simple sentence doesn't contain any dependent clauses, it isn't always short.

- ***Field-based measurements** of these properties, combined with data from laboratory experiments and numerical simulations of LPO development, **form** a framework for interpreting the structure and flow behavior of Earth's upper mantle.*
- *In order to use the ^{10}Be concentrations of our 17 nested catchment samples to interpret spatial patterns in erosion rate, **we used** a spatially-distributed ^{10}Be flux model to compare predicted and measured in situ-produced ^{10}Be concentrations in quartz for four different spatially-distributed erosion scenarios.*

A complex sentence is one with an independent clause and at least one dependent clause.

- *The groundmass is characterized by (1) lath-like feldspars // **that** exhibit anastomosing flow alignment, and (2) alteration of glassy components to clay minerals giving the thin section a cloudy appearance.*
- *Larger, nested catchments have intermediate apparent erosion rates // **that** smoothly integrate the variability found in lower-order tributary samples (Fig. 2A).*

Chapter 7
Conclusions and Acknowledgements

A compound sentence has at least two independent clauses that have related ideas. The two clauses are connected by a comma and a conjunction such as "and", "but", or "so".

* *Beginning at approximately 80 Ma, volcanism in the Sierra Nevada ceased due to flattening of the slab, // **and** deep-seated contractile deformation occurred across the Laramide foreland.*
* *The Elko Formation likely does not encompass the MECO, // **but** this global warming event may be recorded in the Ca 40.45 ± 0.25 Ma tuff of Nelson Creek.*

Exercises

I. Read the following two paragraphs and find out the eight errors contained in the underlined sentences. Each underlined sentence contains only one error. In each case, only one word is involved. You should proofread the sentences and correct the errors.

Conclusions

This contribution resolves some inconsistencies between previous planktic foraminiferal calibrations and in vitro observations, and **1. <u>provides further support for the importance of microenvironment alteration in dictating foraminiferal vital affects.</u>** Our new calibration for Orbulina universa provides one of the most tightly-constrained calibrations of any species to date, **2. <u>which derived from open-ocean samples without risk of artefacts from culture.</u>** Better understanding of foraminiferal autecology and seasonality in the open ocean could in future constrain such calibrations still further. Together with apparently negligible size-fraction or cryptospecies effects in $\delta^{11}B$ and this species' broad geographic range, long fossil record, and large and easily recognizable morphology, **3. <u>this calibration should be prove a very useful tool for reconstruction of past pH and pCO₂.</u>** In addition, through comparison with new and published measurements of other foraminiferal species, **4. <u>an increasingly congruent picture of the nature of foraminiferal vital effects are emerging.</u>** Although ultimately more advanced models of foraminiferal microenvironment alteration and biomineralization—grounded in more extensive physiological and geochemical measurements—are needed, we outline some practical solutions to allow approximation of vital effects in extinct species. These approaches, we suggest, can permit greater confidence in absolute values of ocean pH and atmospheric pCO₂ calculated from the $\delta^{11}B$ of extinct foraminiferal species, thereby extending the utility of the boron isotope-pH proxy.

Acknowledgements

This work was supported by the Natural Environment Research Council (NERC) project "Tempo of Post-glacial Volcanism in Southern Chile" (NE/I013210/5). **5. <u>HR is further supported by grant from the Old Members Trust (University College, Oxford) and Santander Academic Travel Award.</u>** TK is supported by the European Research Council under the European Union's Seventh Framework Program (FP7/2007–2013) / ERC grant agreement number 279925. **6. <u>We greatly appreciative to Steve Wyatt and Phil Holdship for their assistance about the ICPS-</u>**

Chapter 7
Conclusions and Acknowledgements

MS analyses and Nick Marsh for the XRF analyses. We thank Steve Sparks, Lars Hansen, Stephen Turner, Stefan Lachowycz, and **7.** Richard Katz for helpful discussions on various aspects of manuscript. **8.** We also thank Oliver Shorttle and an anonymity reviewer for thorough and constructive reviews which resulted in substantial improvement of this paper, and Mike Bickle for editorial handling. (Henehan, 2016)

II. In the following paragraphs, some sentences are missing. Fill in the blanks with the most suitable ones from the list A–E. There is one extra choice, which does not fit in any of the gaps.

We present evidence that ferropericlase may become interconnected in the lower mantle, leading to reduced viscosity and weakening of CPO. **1.** _____

While our results strongly suggest reduction of CPO due to ferropericlase controlling deformation, results presented here cannot constrain which deformation mechanism is responsible for CPO reduction. Future systematic deformation experiments on bridgmanite-ferropericlase aggregates coupled with in-situ microtomography and/or ex-situ electron microscopy may help to construct deformation maps that can be extrapolated to better constrain likely deformation mechanisms in the lower mantle. **2.** _____ Alternatively, two-phase deformation of lower mantle minerals may be predicted by comprehensive models that allow for not only dislocation slip but also grain nucleation, grain growth, grain-boundary migration, and lattice diffusion creep. In addition, the effects of starting microstructure, strength contrast, and aggregate strain should be looked at more closely. **3.** _____ Future experiments should be done to compare results for samples with different starting microstructures. As shown here, the viscoplastic fast Fourier transform-based approach is a valuable tool for predicting stress and strain partitioning and CPO development in polyphase samples with different starting microstructures. We compare results here to previous studies to examine the role strength contrast between the two-phase plays in determining the deformation-controlling phase and suggest that this may evolve with strain, but more systematic studies are necessary. **4.** _____ (Kaercher et al., 2016)

A. Modeling of two-phase deformation using VPFFT or finite element methods may be best suited for this pursuit as well.

B. Such experiments are becoming increasingly feasible (with larger, more easily recoverable samples) thanks to increased pressure range of large volume presses (T-cups, Drickamer, D-DIA).

C. Results here indicate that temperature did not greatly affect CPO development in two-phase samples, but has a stronger effect on aggregate strength (Fig. 2b).

D. The starting microstructure here had $NaMgF_3$ and NaCl already highly connected.

E. These results reiterate the importance of including the effect of secondary phase ferropericlase on rheology in geophysical models of the lower mantle.

III. Improve the italicized parts in the following sentences to make them more formal and logical.

1. *We have another explanation for* the marine turbidite depositional pattern at site H. The explanation is related to the decreased moisture supply.

2. According to our continental data, temperatures of the lower mid- and low-latitudes were at the present-day level, *or even a few degrees below the present-day level.*

3. In both the Middle and Late Miocene time slice, the higher mid- and high-latitudes were considerably warmer than present, *which does not depend on* prevailing atmospheric pCO_2 conditions.

4. Although *changing plate boundary forces are* less clear-cut than those at the Perth Abyssal Plain microcontinents, *changing plate boundary forces* have also been proposed to have played a role in calving both the Seychelles and Jan Mayen microcontinents.

Chapter 7
Conclusions and Acknowledgements

5. Our results are influenced *by the time of* our experiments early in the melt season: *We can know more* by repeating these tests during or after the monsoon season when the subsurface hydrology *becomes* more developed after sustained large inputs to the system.

6. Earthquakes *whose magnitude can reach* Mw 6.1 around the Davie Ridge and Mw 5.7 around the Europa–Bassas da India Islands *happened* along the fault zone during the last decades.

7. *We do not have access to the actual samples from these studies.* But the chemistry, mineralogy, and preparation procedures are nominally the same *as our own. This suggests* that there is an additional contribution to *the bulk conductivity. This* cannot be accounted for by separately considering the electrical conductivity of olivine and melt.

8. *A self-consistent study would be immensely valuable to the field. In this study,* digital rock physics simulations are supplemented by impedance spectroscopy of the same samples, *similar to Watson & Roberts (2011).*

9. We speculate the existence of a thin, electrochemically distinct layer at the olivine-melt interface. *The layer* might may account for the apparent discrepancy between the bulk electrical conductivities measured and *the bulk electrical conductivities we computed. We computed those* using real partial melt geometries.

10. The electrical conductivity of the deformed sample overlapped the parallel mixing bound (i.e., electrical conduction through parallel pipes). *This* is consistent with deformation-induced melt segregation. *The electrical conductivity of the deformed sample was measured in the shear direction.*

   _____

   _____

11. The Miocene Climate Optimum preceded the MMCT. *The Miocene Climate Optimum has* oscillating but reduced ice volume and high sea level.

   _____

   _____

12. *We compared our results with the results* obtained by Singh et al. (2012). *It indicates* that dissolved Nd concentrations of seawater samples collected in June 2012 are generally 15%–25% lower than *dissolved Nd concentrations* of samples collected in November 2008.

   _____

   _____

References

高原，于华，姜文东. 2019. 研究生学术英语读写教程. 北京：外语教学与研究出版社.

Aktas, H., & San, B. T. (2019). Landslide susceptibility mapping using an automatic sampling algorithm based on two level random sampling. *Computers & Geosciences*, *133*, 104329.

Albert, H., Costa, F., Di Muro, A., Herrin, J., Métrich, N., & Deloule, E. (2019). Magma interactions, crystal mush formation, timescales, and unrest during caldera collapse and lateral eruption at ocean island basaltic volcanoes (Piton de la Fournaise, La Réunion). *Earth and Planetary Science Letters*, *515*, 187–199.

Allabar, A. (2018). Message in a bottle: Spontaneous phase separation of hydrous Vesuvius melt even at low decompression rates. *Earth and Planetary Science Letters*, *501*, 192–201.

Aurell, M., Fregenal-Martínez, M., Bádenas, B., Muñoz-García, M. B., élez, J., Meléndez, N., & de Santisteban, C. (2019). Middle Jurassic–Early Cretaceous tectono-sedimentary evolution of the southwestern Iberian Basin (central Spain): Major palaeogeographical changes in the geotectonic framework of the Western Tethys. *Earth-Science Reviews*, *199*, 102983.

Avice, G., Meier, M. M. M., Marty, B., Wieler, R., Kramers, J. D., Langenhorst, F., Cartigny, P., Maden, C., Zimmermann, L., & Andreoli, M. A. G. (2015). A comprehensive study of noble gases and nitrogen in "Hypatia", a diamond-rich pebble from SW Egypt. *Earth and Planetary Science Letters*, *432*, 243–253.

Bakker, R. R., Frehner, M., & Lupi, M. (2016). How temperature-dependent elasticity alters host rock/magmatic reservoir models: A case study on the effects of ice-cap unloading on shallow volcanic systems. *Earth and Planetary Science Letters*, *456*, 16–25.

Bernhardt, A., Schwanghart, W., Hebbeln, D., Stuut, J. B. W., & Strecker, M. R. (2017).

Immediate propagation of deglacial environmental change to deep-marine turbidite systems along the Chile convergent margin. *Earth and Planetary Science Letters*, *473*, 190–204.

Bezard, R., Gödde, M. F., Hamelin, C., Brennecka, G. A., & Kleine, T. (2016). The effects of magmatic processes and crustal recycling on the molybdenum stable isotopic composition of Mid-Ocean Ridge Basalts. *Earth and Planetary Science Letters, 453*, 171–181.

Brice, L., Baumgartner, L. P., Bouvier, A. S., Kempton, P. D., & Torsten, V. (2018). Multi fluid-flow record during episodic mode Ⅰ opening: A microstructural and SIMS study (Cotiella Thrust Fault, Pyrenees). *Earth and Planetary Science Letters*, *503*, 37–46.

Cao, K., Wang, G. C., Bernet, M., van der Beek, P., & Zhang, K. X. (2015). Exhumation history of the West Kunlun Mountains, northwestern Tibet: Evidence for a long-lived, rejuvenated orogen. *Earth and Planetary Science Letters*, *432*, 391–403.

Caracas, R., Hirose, K., Nomura, R., & Ballmer, M. D. (2019). Melt-crystal density crossover in a deep magma ocean. *Earth and Planetary Science Letters*, *516*, 202–211.

Cargill, M., & Connor, P. O. (2009). *Writing Scientific Research Articles: Strategy and Steps.* London: Wiley-Blackwell.

Carmichael, M. J., Pancost, R. D., & Lunt, D. J. (2018). Changes in the occurrence of extreme precipitation events at the Paleocene–Eocene thermal maximum. *Earth and Planetary Science Letters*, *501*, 24–36.

Cesar, J., Nightingale, M., Becker, V., & Mayer, B. (2020). Stable carbon isotope systematics of methane, ethane and propane from low-permeability hydrocarbon reservoirs. *Chemical Geology*, *558*, 119907.

Chen, Y. X., Schertl, H. P., Zheng, Y, F., Huang, F., Zhou, K., & Gong, Y. Z. (2016). Mg–O isotopes trace the origin of Mg-rich fluids in the deeply subducted continental crust of Western Alps. *Earth and Planetary Science Letters*, *456*, 157–167.

Deville, E., Marsset, T., Courgeon, S., Jatiault, R., Ponte, J. P., Thereau, E., Jouet, G., Jorry, S. J., & Droz, L. (2018). Active fault system across the oceanic lithosphere of the Mozambique Channel: Implications for the Nubia-Somalia southern plate boundary. *Earth and Planetary Science Letters*, *502*, 210–220.

DiBiase, R. A., Denn, A. R., Bierman, P. R., Kirby, E., West, N., & Hidy, A. J. (2018)

Stratigraphic control of landscape response to base-level fall, Young Womans Creek, Pennsylvania, U.S.A. *Earth and Planetary Science Letters*, *456*, 163–173.

Fadlalla, A. H. H. (2019). *Academic Research Writing*. Singapore: Partridge.

Faenza, L., Michelini, A., Crowley, H., Borzi, B., & Faravelli, M. (2020). ShakeDaDO: A data collection combining earthquake building damage and ShakeMap parameters for Italy. *Artificial Intelligence in Geosciences*, *1*, 36–51.

Fouedjio, F. (2020). Exact conditioning of regression random forest for spatial prediction. *Artificial Intelligence in Geosciences*, *1*, 11–23.

Geng, X., Foley, S. F., Liu, Y., Wang, Z., Hu, Z., & Zhou, L. (2019). Thermal-chemical conditions of the North China Mesozoic lithospheric mantle and implication for the lithospheric thinning of cratons. *Earth and Planetary Science Letters*, *516*, 1–11.

Giri, S. J., Swart, P. K., & Pourmand, A. (2019). The influence of seawater calcium ions on coral calcification mechanisms: Constraints from boron and carbon isotopes and B/Ca ratios in Pocillopora damicornis. *Earth and Planetary Science Letters*, *519*, 130–140.

Gong, S., Peng, Y., Bao, H., Feng, D., Cao, X., Crockford, P. W., & Chen, D. (2018). Triple sulfur isotope relationships during sulfate-driven anaerobic oxidation of methane. *Earth and Planetary Science Letters*, *504*, 13–20.

Gourbet, L., Mahéo, G., Shuster, D. L., Tripathy-Lang, A., Leloup, P. H., & Paquette, J. L. (2016). River network evolution as a major control for orogenic exhumation: Case study from the western Tibetan Plateau. *Earth and Planetary Science Letters*, *456*, 168–181.

Gurrola, L. D., & Nicholson, C. (2018). Geomorphic evidence for the geometry and slip rate of a young, low-angle thrust fault: Implications for hazard assessment and fault interaction in complex tectonic environments. *Earth and Planetary Science Letters*, *504*, 198–210.

Hartley, J. (2008). *Academic Writing and Publishing*. New York: Routledge.

Henehan, M. J. (2016). A new boron isotope-pH calibration for Orbulina universa, with implications for understanding and accounting for "vital effects". *Earth and Planetary Science Letters*, *454*, 282–292.

Henry, H., Tilhac, R., Griffin, W. L., O'Reilly, S. Y., Satsukawa, T., Kaczmarek, M. A.,

Grégoire, M., & Ceuleneer, G. (2017). Deformation of mantle pyroxenites provides clues to geodynamic processes in subduction zones: Case study of the Cabo Ortegal Complex, Spain. *Earth and Planetary Science Letters*, *472*, 174–185.

Hood, S. B., Cracknell, M. J., Gazley, M. F., & Reading, A. M. (2019). Improved supervised classification of bedrock in areas of transported overburden: Applying domain expertise at Kerkasha, Eritrea. *Applied Computing and Geosciences*, *3–4*, 100001.

Horgan, H. J., Anderson, B., Alley, R. B., Chamberlain, C. J., Dykes, R., Kehrl, L. M., & Townend, J. (2015). Glacier velocity variability due to rain-induced sliding and cavity formation. *Earth and Planetary Science Letters*, *432*, 273–282.

Hu, R. (2019). Predicted diurnal variation of the deuterium to hydrogen ratio in water at the surface of Mars caused by mass exchange with the regolith. *Earth and Planetary Science Letters*, *519*, 192–201.

Hughes, A., Rood, D. H., Whittaker, A. C., Bell, R. E., Rockwell, T. K., Levy, Y., Wilcken, K. M., Corbett, L. B., Bierman, P. R., DeVecchio, D. E., Marshall, S. T., Gurrola, L. D., & Nicholson, C. (2018). Geomorphic evidence for the geometry and slip rate of a young, low-angle thrust fault: Implications for hazard assessment and fault interaction in complex tectonic environments. *Earth and Planetary Science Letters*, *504*, 198–210.

Hyland, K. (1996). Nurturing hedges in the ESP curriculum. *System, 24*(4), 477–490.

Iacovino, K. (2015). Linking subsurface to surface degassing at active volcanoes: A thermodynamic model with applications to Erebus volcano. *Earth and Planetary Science Letters*, *431*, 59–74.

Johnstone, S. A., Finnegan, N. J., & Hilley, G. E. (2017). Weak bedrock allows north-south elongation of channels in semi-arid landscapes. *Earth and Planetary Science Letters*, *478*, 150–158.

Kaercher, P., Miyagi, L., Kanitpanyacharoen, W., Zepeda-Alarcon, E., Wang, Y., Parkinson, D., Lebensohn, R. A., de Carlo, F., & Wenk, H. R. (2016). Two-phase deformation of lower mantle mineral analogs. *Earth and Planetary Science Letters*, *456*, 134–145.

Kaste, J. M., Lauer, N. E., Spaetzel, A. B., & Goydan, C. (2016). Cosmogenic ^{22}Na as a steady-state tracer of solute transport and water age in first-order catchments. *Earth and Planetary Science Letters*, *456*, 78–86.

References

Kawazoe, T., Nishihara, Y., Ohuchi, T., Miyajima, N., Maruyama, G., Higo, Y., Funakoshi, K., & Irifune, T. (2016). Creep strength of ringwoodite measured at pressure-temperature conditions of the lower part of the mantle transition zone using a deformation-DIA apparatus. *Earth and Planetary Science Letters*, *454*, 10–19.

Lecours, V., Dolan, M. F. J., Micallef, A., & Lucieer, V. L. (2016). A review of marine geomorphometry, the quantitative study of the seafloor. *Hydrology and Earth System Sciences*, *20*(8), 3207–3244.

Li, P., Scott, J. M., Liu, J., & Xia, Q. (2018). Lateral H_2O variation in the Zealandia lithospheric mantle controls orogen width. *Earth and Planetary Science Letters*, *502*, 200–209.

Lopez, G. I. (2015). Dissolved and particulate ^{230}Th–^{232}Th in the Central Equatorial Pacific Ocean: Evidence for far-field transport of the East Pacific Rise hydrothermal plume. *Earth and Planetary Science Letters*, *431*, 87–95.

Ma, C., Meyers, S. R., & Sageman, B. B. (2019). Testing Late Cretaceous astronomical solutions in a 15-million-year astrochronologic record from North America. *Earth and Planetary Science Letters*, *513*, 1–11.

Magrini, F., Jozinović, D., Cammarano, F., Michelini, A., & Boschi, L. (2020). Local earthquakes detection: A benchmark dataset of 3-component seismograms built on a global scale. *Artificial Intelligence in Geosciences*, *1*, 1–10.

Miles, K. E., Hubbard, B., Quincey, D. J., Miles, E. S., Irvine-Fynn, T. D. L., & Rowan, A. V. (2019). Surface and subsurface hydrology of debris-covered Khumbu Glacier, Nepal, revealed by dye tracing. *Earth and Planetary Science Letters*, *513*, 176–186.

Miller, K. J., Montési, L. G. J., & Zhu, W. (2015). Estimates of olivine-basaltic melt electrical conductivity using a digital rock physics approach. *Earth and Planetary Science Letters*, *432*, 332–341.

Morison, A. (2019). Timescale of overturn in a magma ocean cumulate. *Earth and Planetary Science Letters*, *516*, 25–36.

Park, Y., Yoo, H. J., Lee, W. S., Lee, C. K., Lee, J., Park, H., Kim, J., & Kim, Y. (2015). P-wave velocity structure beneath Mt. Melbourne in northern Victoria Land, Antarctica: Evidence of partial melting and volcanic magma sources. *Earth and Planetary Science Letters*, *432*, 293–299.

Parthasarathy, G., Pandey, O. P., Sreedhar, B., Sharma, M., Tripathi, P., & Vedanti, N. (2019). First observation of microspherule from the infratrappean Gondwana sediments below Killari region of Deccan LIP, Maharashtra (India) and possible implications. *Geoscience Frontiers*, *10*(6), 2281–2285.

Pierce, E. L., van de Flierdt, T., Williams, T., Hemming, S. R., Cook, C. P., & Passchier, S. (2017). Evidence for a dynamic East Antarctic ice sheet during the mid-Miocene climate transition. *Earth and Planetary Science Letters*, *478*, 1–13.

Rampino, M. R., & Caldeira, K. (2020). A 32-million-year cycle detected in sea-level fluctuations over the last 545 Myr. *Geoscience Frontiers*, *11*(6), 2061–2065.

Rondet, M., Martel, C., & Bourdier, J. L. (2019). The intermediate step in fractionation trends of mildly alkaline volcanic suites: An experimental insight from the Pavin trachyandesite (Massif Central, France). *Comptes Rendus Geoscience*, *351*(8), 525–539.

Salvioli-Mariani, E., Boschetti, T., Toscani, L., Montanini, A., Petriglieri, J. R., & Bersani, D. (2020). Multi-stage rodingitization of ophiolitic bodies from Northern Apennines (Italy): Constraints from petrography, geochemistry and thermodynamic modelling. *Geoscience Frontiers*, *11*(6), 2103–2125.

Schmidt, A., Pourteau, A., Candan, O., & Oberhänsli, R. (2015). Lu–Hf geochronology on cm-sized garnets using microsampling: New constraints on garnet growth rates and duration of metamorphism during continental collision (Menderes Massif, Turkey). *Earth and Planetary Science Letters*, *432*, 24–35.

Smith, M. E., Cassel, E. J., Jicha, B. R., Singer, B. S., & Canada, A. S. (2017). Hinterland drainage closure and lake formation in response to Middle Eocene Farallon slab removal, Nevada, U.S.A. *Earth and Planetary Science Letters*, *479*, 156–169.

Stewart, J. A., Gutjahr, M., James, R. H., Anand, P., & Wilson, P. A. (2016). Influence of the Amazon River on the Nd isotope composition of deep water in the western equatorial Atlantic during the Oligocene–Miocene transition. *Earth and Planetary Science Letters*, *454*, 132–141.

Stow, D., Nicholson, U., Kearsey, S., Tatum, D., Gardiner, A., Ghabra, A., & Jaweesh, M. (2020). The Pliocene-Recent Euphrates river system: Sediment facies and architecture as an analogue for subsurface reservoirs. *Energy Geoscience*, *1*(3–4), 174–193.

Sumbane-Prinsloo, L., Bunt, J., Matjie, R., Piketh, S., Neomagus, H., & Waanders, F. (2020).

The effect of particle size on the pollution reduction potential of a South African coal-derived low-smoke fuel. *Energy Geoscience*, *1*(3–4), 165–173.

Swales, J. M., & Feak, C. B. (2004). *Academic Writing for Graduates Students* (2nd ed.). Ann Arbor: University of Michigan Press.

Tielke, J. A., Zimmerman, M. E., & Kohlstedt, D. L. (2016). Direct shear of olivine single crystals. *Earth and Planetary Science Letters, 455,* 140–148.

Ustra, A., Mendonça, C., Leite, A., Jaqueto, P., & Novello, V. F. (2019). Low field frequency dependent magnetic susceptibility inversion. *Computers & Geosciences*, *133*, 104326.

Valdez-Grijalva, M. A., Muxworthy, A. R., Williams, W., Ó Conbhuí, P., Nagy, L., Roberts, A. P., & Heslop, D. (2018). Magnetic vortex effects on first-order reversal curve (FORC) diagrams for greigite dispersions. *Earth and Planetary Science Letters*, *501*, 103–111.

Whittaker, J. M., Williams, S. E., Halpin, J. A., Wild, T. J., Stilwell, J. D., Jourdan, F., & Daczko, N. R. (2016). Eastern Indian Ocean microcontinent formation driven by plate motion changes. *Earth and Planetary Science Letters*, *454*, 203–212.

Zhao, Z., Wu, K., Fan, Y., Guo, J., Zeng, B., & Yue, W. (2020). An optimization model for conductivity of hydraulic fracture networks in the Longmaxi shale, Sichuan Basin, Southwest China. *Energy Geoscience*, *1*(1–2), 47–54.

Zou, S., Chen, X., Xu, D., Brzozowski, M. J., Lai, F., Bian, Y., Wang, Z., & Deng, T. (2021). A machine learning approach to tracking crustal thickness variations in the eastern North China Craton. *Geoscience Frontiers*, *12*(5), 101195.

Appendix I Frequently-used Collocations in Geoscience Papers

A collocation has two or more words that often go together. These combinations are more likely to be accepted by native speakers. In geoscience papers, there are also a lot of collocations that can be accepted by researchers in this field. Four types of collocations are widely used and their examples are listed below. Try to use them correctly, so as to make your scientific writing more understandable.

adjective + noun

abaxial leaf	背面叶
abiotic apatite	非生物磷灰石
abnormal sensor current	传感器电流异常
abrupt increase	突然增加
abundant empirical evidence	丰富的实验证据
abundant impurity	大量杂质
acetic aid	醋酸
acid neutral fraction	酸性中性馏分
active volcano	活火山
additional illumination	额外的照明
additional overburden	额外的负担
additional sample	附加样本
additional slip plane	附加滑移面
adjacent basin	邻近的盆地
adjacent hydrographic measurement	邻近水文测量
adjacent region	邻近地区
adjacent unit	相邻单元
aeromagnetic data	航磁数据
alternative possibility	替代可能性
ambient borate	周边硼酸盐
ambient level	环境水平

ambient seawater	周边海水
amorphous carbon rich lithology	无定形富碳岩性
analytical inaccuracy	分析误差
analytical parameter	分析参数
analytical procedure	分析程序
analytical reproducibility	分析重现性
analytical spot	分析点
ancient atmosphere	古老大气层
anhydrous condition	无水状态
anisotropic result	各向异性结果
anisotropic viscosity	各向异性黏度
anomalous measurement	异常测量
anomalous result	异常结果
anonymous reviewer	匿名审稿人
anthropogenic carbon emission	人为碳排放
aperture size	孔径大小
apparent discrepancy	明显差异
aquatic contribution	水生贡献
aqueous borate ion	硼酸根离子水溶液
areal density of stomata	气孔面积密度
arid environment	干旱环境
artificial structure	人工结构
asthenospheric condition	软流圈条件
asthenospheric mantle	软流圈地幔
asthenospheric upper mantle	软流圈上地幔
atmospheric carbon	大气碳
atmospheric entry	大气入口
atmospheric gas	大气
atmospheric noble gas	大气稀有气体
atmospheric value	大气值
atmospheric variability	大气变化率
available data	可用数据
basal age	基础年龄
basaltic rock	玄武岩
basinal sedimentary	盆地沉积
benthic foraminifera	底栖有孔虫

Appendix I Frequently-used Collocations in Geoscience Papers

benthic species	底栖物种
binocular microscope	双目显微镜
biogenic carbon	生物碳
biostratigraphic indicator	生物地层指标
biotic calcite	生物方解石
black shale	黑色页岩
boric acid	硼酸
brittle and plastic behavior	脆性和塑性行为
bulk sample	大块样品
bulk sedimentary	大块状沉积物
calcareous shale	钙质页岩
carbonaceous chondrite	碳质球粒陨石
cautionary example	警示示例
Cenozoic volcanic rock age	新生代火山岩年龄
chemical composition range	化学成分范围
chemical diffusion	化学扩散
chemical nature	化学性质
chemical weathering	化学风化
chondritic insoluble organic matter	球粒装不可溶有机物
chronological uncertainty	时间不确定性
chronostratigraphic framework	年代地层结构
clastic sediment	碎屑沉积物
clastic sedimentary rock	碎屑沉积岩
climatic threshold	气候阈值
close morphological resemblance	闭合形态相似
coastal region	沿海地区
colloidal silica	胶体二氧化硅
cometary matter	彗星物质
cometary origin	彗星起源
compositional gradient	成分梯度
comprehensive dataset	综合数据集
compressional deformation	压缩变形
compressional structure	压缩结构
compressive creep experiment	压缩蠕变实验
compressive stress	压应力
considerable variability	相当大的可变性

consistent convergence	一致趋同
constitutive equation	组成方程
constitutive mineral	组成矿物
constitutive relationship	组成关系
constructive comment	建设性意见
contemporary volcanism	当代火山活动
continental crust	大陆地壳
continental subduction channel	大陆俯冲通道
continuous exhumation	持续发掘
continuous recording	连续记载
continuous seismic data	连续地震数据
convective removal	对流清除
core suggestion	核心建议
cosmogenic noble gas	宇宙稀有气体
cosmogenic radionuclide data	宇宙成因放射性核素数据
crustal and topographic feature	晶体和地形特征
crustal architecture	地壳建筑
crustal assemblage	地壳组合
crustal column	地壳柱
crustal deformation	地壳变形
crustal material	地壳物质
crustal thickness	地壳厚度
crystal lattice	水晶格子
crystallographic axis	结晶轴
crystallographic orientation	晶体取向
crystallographic plane	晶面
crystallographic reference	晶体学参考
current high topography	当前高地势
current size	现有规模
current study	当前研究
cylindrical correction	圆柱校正
dateable mineral	可测年代的矿物
deep basal cavity	深基底腔
deep lithosphere architecture	深层岩石圈结构
deep ocean and atmosphere	深海和大气
depositional age	沉积年代

Appendix I Frequently-used Collocations in Geoscience Papers

depositional environment	沉积环境
depositional sequence	沉积序列
detrital geo-thermochronologic analysis	分散地热年代分析
detrital zircon	碎屑锆石
diagenetic alteration history	成岩蚀变史
diagenetic fluid	成岩流体
diagenetic recrystallization	成岩重结晶
different degrees	不同程度
different elevations	不同标高
different hydrous minerals	不同的含水矿物
different magnitudes	不同幅度
different patterns	不同模式
different plant species	不同的植物种类
different rims	不同轮辋
different thicknesses	不同厚度
different tissue types	不同的组织类型
diffusive boundary layer	扩散边界层
diffusive pathway	扩散途径
diffusive profile	扩散轮廓
direct evidence	直接证据
direct impact	直接影响
direct measurement	直接测量
direct shear geometry	直剪几何
distinct peristomatal rim	明显的气孔缘环
distinct phase	截然不同的阶段
distinguishable morphology	可区分的形态
dominant canopy component	主要冠层成分
dominant dislocation	显性错位
dominant slip system	主导滑移系统
ductile property	延展性
dynamic simulation	动态模拟
earlier collision	早期碰撞
earlier version	早期版本
early diagenesis	早期成岩作用
eastward crustal extrusion	地壳向东挤压
electrical conductivity	电导率

electrical pulse	电脉冲
elemental combustion system	元素燃烧系统
elemental ratio	元素比例
enigmatic pebble	神秘的卵石
environmental factor	环境因素
environmental signal	环境信号
environmental stimuli	环境刺激
environmental variable	环境变量
environmental variation	环境变化
epicentral distance	震中距离
epidermal cell	表皮细胞
epidermal cell density	表皮细胞密度
epitactic orientation relationship	外部取向关系
equivalent spherical radius	等量球半径
equivalent strain rate	等效应变率
equivalent stress	等效应力
equivalent value	等效值
erosional exhumation	侵蚀剥落
evaporitic sediment	蒸发沉积物
evolutionary history	进化史
exponential creep equation	指数蠕变方程
exponential law component	指数律成分
exponential regime	指数制度
extensive exhumation	深度发掘
extensive tectonism	深度构造
external detector	外部检测器
external fluid	外部流体
external inflow	外部流入
external reproducibility	外部再现性
extinct species	已灭绝的物种
extraterrestrial material	宇宙物质
extraterrestrial nature	宇宙特征
extraterrestrial object	宇宙物体
extreme moisture deficit	极度缺水
fluid inclusion study	流体包裹体研究
fluvial and lacustrine sediment	河湖沉积物

Appendix I   Frequently-used Collocations in Geoscience Papers

fluvial sandstone	河流砂岩
foraminiferal calcite	有孔虫方解石
foraminiferal carbonate	有孔虫碳酸盐
foraminiferal test	有孔虫试验
formic acid	甲酸
fruitful discussion	富有成果的讨论
fumarolic activity	气流活动
future research	未来的研究
gametogenic calcite	配子方解石
generational turnover	代际更替
genetic link	遗传联系
genotypic trait evolution	基因型性状进化
geochemical feature	地球化学特征
geochemical proxy system	地球化学代理系统
geochemical reservoir	地球化学储层
geochemical signature	地球化学特征
geodynamic mechanism	地球动力学机制
geodynamic model	地球动力学模型
geographic range	地理范围
geographical distribution	地域分布
geological and seismological studies	地质和地震学
geological context	地质背景
geological information	地质信息
geological observation	地质观察
geological setting	地质环境
geological sketch map	地质示意图
geological survey	地质调查
geological timescale	地质时间尺度
geometric alpha-ejection correction	几何阿尔法喷射校正
geometric correction	几何校正
geophysical observation	地球物理观测
geothermal activity	地热活动
geothermal gradient	地热梯度
glacial and interglacial state/time	冰川和间冰期
glacial and submarine volcanic rock	冰川和海底火山岩
glacial expansion	冰川扩张

glacial movement	冰川运动
glacial termination	冰川终止
global climatic consequence	全球气候变化后果
good analogy	恰当的类比
good representation	有代表性
gradual ecosystem response	渐进的生态系统反应
granitic gneiss	花岗片麻岩
granitic magma	花岗岩岩浆
granitic protolith	花岗原生岩
gravitational potential energy	重力势能
greater dispersion	较大面积分散
greater fraction	较大的比重
heavier isotope	较重的同位素
heavy and light nitrogen	重氮和轻氮
helpful comment	有用的评论
heterogeneous metasomatism	异质交代作用
high dispersion	高分散
higher density	更高的密度
highest load step	最高负载阶跃
historical leaf	历史叶子
hydrographic measurement	水文测量
ideal region	理想区域
identical major element	相同的主要元素
identical thermal history	相同的热历史
identical treatment principle	相同的处理原则
identical value	相同的价值
igneous apatite	火成磷灰石
immediate vicinity	邻近地区
important element	重要元素
important geochemical tracer	重要的地球化学示踪剂
important implication	重要意义
important microphysical process	重要的微物理过程
important parameter	重要参数
independent evidence	独立证据
independent mechanism	独立机制
independent rotational axe	独立旋转轴

Appendix I Frequently-used Collocations in Geoscience Papers

indigenous component	本土成分
individual detrital zircon	单个碎屑锆石
individual dislocation slip system	个别脱位滑移系统
individual measurement	单独测量
individual sample	个别样本
initial diagenesis	初始成岩作用
initial model	初始模型
inorganic calcite	无机方解石
inorganic carbon	无机碳
inorganic precipitation experiment	无机沉淀实验
insightful comment	有见地的评论
insufficient data	数据不足
insufficient resolution	分辨率不足
intensive study	强化学习
intercellular carbon	细胞间碳
internal climate feedback	内部气候反馈
ionic species	离子种类
isotopic analysis	同位素分析
isotopic composition	同位素成分
isotopic disequilibrium	同位素不平衡
isotopic fractionation	同位素分馏
isotopic ration	同位素比
kinetic energy	动能
large bolide	大型火流星
large composite basin	大型复合盆地
large conodont	大牙形石
large genome size	大基因组
large global temperature rise	全球气温大幅上升
larger epidermal cell	较大的表皮细胞
largest orogenic highland	最大的造山带
latter observation	后期观察
light availability	可用光
light condition	光照条件
light level	亮度
light stable isotope	光稳定同位素
liquid nitrogen temperature	液氮温度

lithospheric cause	岩石圈成因
lithospheric condition	岩石圈条件
lithospheric mantle	岩石圈地幔
lithospheric root	岩石圈根部
lithospheric wedge model	岩石圈楔形模型
local decompression	局部减压
local ecology	当地生态
local moisture	局部水分
local shallow structure	局部浅层构造
local signal	本地信号
long timescale	长时间
low metabolic rate	代谢率低
low parameter	低参数
low stress	低压
low temperature	低温
low value	低价值
lower crustal	下地壳
lower mantle	下地幔
lower ration	低量配给
magmatic activity	岩浆活动
magmatic belt	岩浆带
magmatic domain	岩浆域
magmatic fluid	岩浆液
magmatic history	岩浆史
magmatic rock	岩浆岩
magmatic zircon	岩浆锆石
magnetic polarity	磁极性
magnetic reversal	磁反转
magnetostratigraphic correlation	磁地层相关性
magnetostratigraphic result	磁地层结果
main component	主要成分
major structure and topography	主要结构和地形
marine sediment	海洋沉积物
marine sedimentary rock	海洋沉积岩
marine temperature	海洋温度
mass redistribution	大规模再分配

Appendix I Frequently-used Collocations in Geoscience Papers

maximum burial temperature	最高埋藏温度
maximum conductance	最大电导
maximum extent	最大程度
maximum temperature	最高温度
mean value	平均值
meaningful information	有意义的信息
mechanical behavior	机械性能
mechanistic understanding	机械的理解
metabolic process	代谢过程
metamorphic age	变质年代
metamorphic basement	变质基底
metamorphic dehydration	变质脱水
metamorphic domain	变质域
metamorphic fluid	变质流体
metamorphic growth zone	变质生长带
metamorphic origin	变质起源
metamorphic rock	变质岩
metasomatic fluid	交代体液
meteoritic class	陨石级
meteoritic lithology	陨石岩性
meteoritic material	陨石物质
micritic limestone	微晶石灰岩
micromorphological parameter	微形态参数
micromorphological property	微观形态特性
microstructural analyse	微观结构分析
microstructural observation	微观结构观察
mineral distribution	矿物分布
minor component	次要成分
minor influence	轻微影响
minor rotation	轻微旋转
minor subcanopy component	微型的亚冠层组件
molecular ratio	分子比
monometamorphic complex	单变态复合体
morphologic component	形态成分
morphologic term	形态学术语
morphological measurement	形态测量

morphological property	形态特性
morphological similarity	形态相似
morphological trait	形态特征
narrow band	窄带
narrow peak	窄峰
natural biogenic precipitation	自然生物沉淀
negative feedback	负面反馈
negative value	负值
new correlation	新的相关性
new zircon	新锆石
noble gas	稀有气体
normal polarity	正常极性
northern and southern unit	南北单元
northern boundary	北部边界
northern limb	北翼
northward subduction	向北俯冲
northwest direction	西北方向
numerical simulation	数值模拟
numerous environmental parameters	众多环境参数
obvious impact	明显的影响
oceanic lithosphere	海洋岩石圈
oceanic mantle	海洋地幔
oceanic remnant	海洋遗迹
oceanic slab	大洋板
oceanographic data	海洋数据
ontogenetic migration	本体迁移
opening time fraction	开放时间段
operational conductance	操作电导
operational rate	运作率
optimal climatic range	最佳气候范围
optimal photosynthetic rate	最佳光合速率
optimal range	最佳范围
orbital configuration	轨道配置
ordinary chondrite	普通球粒陨石
organic material	有机物质
organic metamorphism	有机变质

Appendix I Frequently-used Collocations in Geoscience Papers

orogenic belt	造山带
orogenic process	造山过程
orogenic history	造山史
paleogeographic reconstruction	古地理重建
partial zone	部分区域
peak temperature	峰值温度
peripheral foreland basin	外围前陆盆地
petrogenetic model	成岩模型
petrological and geochemical observation	岩石地球化学观测
petrological thermobarometry	岩石热压法
phenotypic change	表型改变
photosynthetic activity	光合活性
photosynthetic carbon	光合碳
photosynthetic compensation	光合补偿
photosynthetic process	光合作用过程
photosynthetic rate	光合速率
photosynthetic symbiont	光合共生体
phreatomagmatic explosion crater	岩浆喷发口
physical parameter	物理参数
physical property	物理特性
physiological change	生理变化
physiological response	生理反应
planktic foraminifera	浮游孔虫
plastic leaf phenotype	塑性叶表型
plausible geodynamic explanation	合理的地球动力学解释
polymetamorphic complex	多变态复合物
poor crystallinity	结晶度差
positive bias	正偏向
positive feedback	正面反馈
positive topography	正地形
positive value	正值
post-depositional temperature	沉积后的温度
post-formative ejecta	后期形成喷射物
potential disintegration	有解体可能性
potential geological implication	潜在的地质意义
potential impact	潜在影响

potential source	潜在来源
potential target	潜在目标
present dataset	当前数据集
present study	当前研究
previous conodont	早期牙形石
previous diffusion experiment	先前的扩散实验
previous estimate	先前的估计
previous interpretation	前述解释
previous leaf generation	前叶世代
primary source	主要来源
primitive achondrite group	原始无球粒陨石群
principal component analysis	主要成分分析
prominent feature	突出特点
pyroclastic infill	火山碎屑岩
quantitative estimate	定量估计
quantitative palaeoecological signal	定量古生态信号
radioactive decay	放射性衰变
real value	实际价值
recent eruption	最近喷发
recent revision	近期修订
recognizable morphology	可识别的形态
red line	红线
regional correlation	区域相关性
regional crustal structure	区域地壳结构
regional difference	区域差异
regional exhumation	区域发掘
regional sedimentary	区域性沉积
regional vegetation	区域植被
regular epidermal cell	常规表皮细胞
regular knot	常规结
relative elemental abundance	相对元素丰度
relative strength	相对强度
relative travel time	相对传输时间
relative value	相对价值
relative velocity structure	相对速度结构
reliable concentration	可靠浓度

Appendix I Frequently-used Collocations in Geoscience Papers

remote mountain	偏远山区
representative example	有代表性的例子
reproducible data	可复制数据
reproducible subset	可复制子集
residual time	剩余时间
rheological behavior	流变行为
rheological regime	流变状态
robust difference	稳健差异
same mechanistic response	相同的机械反应
schematic diagram	示意图
schematic visualization	示意图可视化
secondary encrustation	二次结壳
sedimentary provenance	沉积物源
seismic array	地震阵列
seismic network	地震台网
seismic reflection data	地震反射数据
seismic station	地震台
seismic wave	地震波
selective process	选择过程
semi-quantitative indicator	半定量指标
significant contribution	显著贡献
significant correlation	显著相关
significant deviation	显著偏差
significant dextral transpression	明显的右旋挤压
significant fractionation	显著分馏
significant overlap	显著重叠
similar bedrock	类似的基岩
similar span	相似跨度
similar temperature sensitivity range	相似的温度灵敏度范围
simultaneous exhumation	同时发掘
single conodont element	单牙形元素
single crystal	单晶
single limestone sample	单个石灰石样品
sizeable blank correction	大量空白校正
slowest diffusing species	扩散最慢的物种
small crystal	小型晶体

small crystallite size	微晶尺寸
small scale	小规模
small structure	小型结构
smaller volume estimate	较小的体积估算
solar system	太阳系
solid line	实线
southern basin	南部盆地
southern margin	南缘
southern tip	南端
spatial distribution	空间分布
spatial occurrence	空间发生
specific age peak	特定年龄峰值
specific crystallographic axe	特定结晶轴
specific morphotype	特定形态
specific slip system	特定滑移系统
specific source	具体来源
stable isotope	稳定同位素
static peak	静态峰值
steady exhumation	持续发掘
stepwise extraction	逐步提取
stepwise manner	循序渐进
stomatal density	气孔密度
stomatal index	气孔指数
stomatal scale	气孔大小
straightforward explanation	简明的解释
stratigraphic age	地层年代
stratigraphic column	地层柱
stratigraphic log	地层日志
strong morphological similarity	形态相似性强
strong negative correlation	强负相关
structural and morphotectonic analysis	结构和形态构造分析
structural section	结构截面
suboptimal range	次优范围
subsequent generation	后代
substantial temperature rise	温度大幅上升
substantial underestimate	严重低估

Appendix I Frequently-used Collocations in Geoscience Papers

subtropical environment	亚热带环境
successive leaf generation	连续叶生成
sufficient precision	足够的精度
supracrustal rock	地壳上岩
surficial adsorption	表面吸附
syndepositional volcanism	沉积性火山作用
synorogenic sediment	共生沉积物
synthetic diamond	合成钻石
synthetic target	合成目标
systematic bias	系统偏差
systematic correlation	系统相关
systematic difference	系统差异
taxonomic identification	分类鉴定
tectonic evolution	构造演化
tectonic feature	构造特征
tectonic surface	构造面
teleseismic data	远震数据
teleseismic receiver	远震接收机
temporal resolution	时间分辨率
temporal variation	时间变化
terrestrial and shallow marine deposition	陆地和浅海沉积
terrestrial atmospheric pattern	地球大气模式
terrestrial contamination	陆地污染
terrestrial deposit	陆地沉积
terrestrial ecosystem	陆地生态系统
terrestrial environmental change	陆地环境变化
terrestrial leaf matter	陆地叶片
terrestrial leaf wax	陆地叶蜡
terrestrial organic carbon	陆地有机碳
terrestrial origin	陆地起源
terrestrial record	地面记录
terrestrial rock	陆地岩石
terrestrial sample	陆地样本
terrestrial sediment	陆地沉积物
terrestrial sedimentary rock	陆地沉积岩
theoretical travel time	理论传输时间

thermal diffusion	热扩散
thermal energy	热能
thermal evolution	热演化
thermal history	热历史
tomographic image	断层扫描图像
tomographic inversion	断层扫描反演
tomographic method	断层扫描法
topographic development	地形发展
topographic evolution	地形演变
topographic height	地形高度
topographic unit	地形单位
total alkalinity	总碱度
total extraction	总萃取量
traditional bootstrap	传统引导
triaxial compression experiment	三轴压缩实验
turbulent flow	湍流
twin configuration	孪生结构
typical continental subduction	典型的大陆俯冲
typical lithospheric stress	典型的岩石圈应力
typical local silicate	典型的局部硅酸盐
typical mineral assemblage	典型的矿物组合
ubiquitous component phase	普遍的成分阶段
ultramafic intrusion	超基性岩体
ultravolatile element	超挥发性元素
uneven representation	代表不均
uniaxial or triaxial compression	单轴或三轴压缩
unradiogenic limestone	非放射性石灰石
upper limit	上限
upper mantle	上地幔
useful tracer	有效示踪剂
valuable discussion	有价值的讨论
variable concentration	可变浓度
variable proportion	可变比例
variable size	可变尺寸
variable temperature and salinity	可变的温度和盐度
various angles	各种角度

Appendix I Frequently-used Collocations in Geoscience Papers

various controlled experiments	各种对照实验
various leaf properties	各种叶片特性
vertical extrusion	垂直挤压
vertical profile	垂直轮廓
vertical structure	垂直结构
viable boron	活性硼
viable source	可靠的来源
visible example	明显的例子
visual inspection	肉眼观察
visual qualification	视觉鉴定
vital effect	重要作用
volatile element	挥发性元素
volcanic activity	火山活动
volcanic arc	火山弧
volcanic ash layer	火山灰层
volcanic event	火山事件
volcanic field	火山地带
volcanic magma source	火山岩浆源
volcanic origin	火山成因
volcanic rock	火山岩
volcanogenic zircon	火山锆石
weak retrogression	弱回归
western edge	西缘
widespread coeval deposition	大面积同期沉积
young peak	新生高峰

adverb + adjective

apparently negligible	显然可以忽略不计的
approximately equal	大致相等的
bimonthly hydrographic	双月进行的水文的
broadly compatible	广泛兼容的
certainly shorter	肯定更短的
comparatively scarce	比较稀缺的
considerably higher	相当高的
considerably large	相当大的

consistently low	持续走低的
directly analogous	直接类似的
easily distinguishable	容易区分的
easily recognizable	容易识别的
ecologically analogous	生态上相似的
essentially identical	本质上相同的
essentially pure	基本纯净的
extremely heavy	非常沉重的
extremely high	非常高的
extremely rare	非常稀有的
freshly exposed	刚刚暴露的
fully compatible	完全兼容的
fully quantifiable	完全可量化的
fully reset	完全重置的
fundamentally well-founded	基本上是有根据的
generally consistent	大体一致的
geographically widespread	地域广泛的
geologically unreasonable	地质上不合理的
highly dispersed	高度分散的
highly monsoonal	强季风的
highly variable	高度变化的
increasingly congruent	越来越一致的
insufficiently unusual	异常不足的
internally consistent	内部一致的
intrinsically difficult	本质上很难的
isotopically similar	同位素相似的
largely consistent	基本上一致的
likely negligible	可忽略的
markedly different	显著不同的
merely facultative	仅具有兼容性的
mostly euhedral	大部分为自形的
mostly peraluminous	多数过铝的
mostly similar	大体相似的

Appendix I Frequently-used Collocations in Geoscience Papers

nearly identical	几乎相同的
partially reset	部分重置的
particularly low	特别低的
particularly rich	特别富足的
partly attributable	部分归因的
physiologically analogous	生理上类似的
relatively consistent	相对一致的
remarkably homogeneous	极其同质化的
roughly equal	大致相等的
roughly simultaneous	大致同时的
specifically contemporaneous	特别是同时期的
statistically significant	具有统计意义的
strikingly similar	惊人相似的
strongly biased	非常有倾向性的
strongly dependent	强烈依赖的
substantially younger	年轻得多的
sufficiently high	足够高的
tectonically lower	构造低的
unrealistically low	低得离谱的
unreasonably long	漫长的

adverb + verb

accurately locate	准确定位
accurately simulate	准确模拟
accurately trace	准确追踪
alternatively protract	交替拖延
approximately commence	大约……开始
be apparently sourced	显然来自……
be carefully controlled	被精细控制
be clearly resolved	尚未明确解决
be clearly shown	清楚地显示
be commonly characterized	通常具有……特征
be commonly explained	通常被解释为
be commonly observed	通常可被观察到

be commonly used	通常被用于
be considered environmentally	被认为对环境有……作用
be episodically interrupted	偶然被中断了
be essentially trapped	本质上受困于
be fairly well understood	可以很好被理解
be generally accepted	被普遍接受
be genetically linked	有遗传联系
be largely inherited	在很大程度上被继承
be likely reactivated	可能已被重新激活
be not evenly distributed	分布不均
be optimally located	位于最佳位置
be preferentially sampled	被优先采样
be primarily controlled	主要受控于
be primarily influenced	主要受到……影响
be repeatedly processed	被反复加工
be roughly located	大致位于
be sequentially analyzed	被依次分析
be strongly supported	被强烈支持
be subsequently criticized by	随后遭到了批评
be subsequently split into	随后被分为
be unevenly distributed	分布不均
be widely used	被广泛使用
briefly summarize	简要总结
cannot be easily derived	不能轻易得出
cannot be independently measured	不能被独立测量
chemically and isotopically fractionate	化学和同位素分馏
clearly reveal	清楚地揭示
closely relate	密切相关
closely resemble	非常相似
completely disaggregate	完全分解
conservatively assume	保守地假设
considerably offset	大大抵消
consistently show	始终显示
definitively associate	明确地联系
directly decide	直接决定

Appendix I Frequently-used Collocations in Geoscience Papers

effectively respond	有效回应
effectively restrict	有效限制
equivocally interpret	模棱两可地解释
fully propagate	充分传播
greatly deviate	严重偏离
irreversibly change	不可逆转地改变
iteratively solve	迭代地解决
mainly consist of	主要包括
mainly correspond to	主要回应
mainly focus on	主要集中在
moderately metamorphose	适度变形/变态
mostly show	大多数情况下表示
necessarily exclude	必然排除
necessarily imply	必然暗示
originally include	最初包括
partially match	部分匹配
partly accommodate	部分容纳
possibly provide	可能提供
possibly suggest	可能暗示
potentially provide	可能提供
potentially reflect	可能反映出
primarily originate	主要起源于
primarily reflect	主要反映
probably initiate	可能发起
probably occur	可能发生
probably reside in	可能居住
properly resolve	妥善解决
randomly generate	随机产生
rarely preserve	很少保存
significantly raise	大幅度提高
simultaneously activate	同时激活
simultaneously explore	同时探索
slightly accelerate	略有加速
sporadically occur	偶尔发生
structurally correlate	结构上相关

tentatively apply	暂时适用
tentatively suggest	暂时建议
tightly constrain	严格约束
undoubtedly confirm and strengthen	无疑证实和加强
unequivocally show	明确显示
visually inspect	用肉眼观察

verb + adverb

come vertically	垂直进入
consist essentially of	本质上包括
depend on strongly	强烈依靠
differ from significantly	差异很大
exhume slowly	慢慢发掘
extend spatially	空间延伸
flow laterally	横向流动
last approximately	大约持续……
occur primarily	主要发生
operate simultaneously	同时操作
produce directly	直接生产
vary systematically	系统地变化

Appendix II Keys to Exercises

Chapter 1

I.

1. in	2. on	3. for	4. of	5. of; for
6. During; in	7. at	8. with	9. to	10. at

II.

Paragraph One

1. a	2. the	3. Ø	4. the	5. Ø
6. Ø	7. Ø	8. the	9. Ø	10. Ø

Paragraph Two

1. the	2. the	3. Ø	4. a	5. The
6. the	7. the	8. The	9. the	10. Ø

Chapter 2

I.

1. using	2. enhanced	3. accelerated	4. collected

II.

1. is usually described   2. compared

3. Areas with significant relief   4. occurred

III.

    1. D   2. A   3. B   4. E

IV.

    4. A   8. B

Chapter 3

I.

1. We infer that this thrust belt probably reactivated the Paleozoic Kudi suture, given their similar trace in map view (Fig. 1).

2. Stomatal density (SD) and stomatal index (SI) in fossil Litsea calicarioides leaves reveal large changes that are coincident with the three phases identified by the carbon isotope values (Fig. 4).

3. Although the Antarctic Ice Sheet is estimated to have melted from ~125% to ~50% of its modern size, there is thus far no evidence for an increase in atmospheric CO_2 associated with the Mi-1 glacial termination in the earliest Miocene.

4. To the southwest, the Tianshuihai–Karakoram terranes have been sliced by the Karakorum fault, along which the Baltoro batholith intruded at 26–15 Ma.

5. As a result, plates that share an interlocking ridge-transform plate boundary show a degree of coupling.

6. It is evident that leaf physiology and phenotype are the results of numerous environmental parameters, including Ca.

7. Current theory concerning the leaf physiological response over millennial timescales supports our interpretation that the reduction of $g_{c[max]}$ from Phase 1 to Phase 2, and subsequent increase from Phase 2 to Phase 3 (Fig. 4), can reflect an increase in Ca during the ~20 kyr period comprising Phase 2.

8. In this case, the rift zone is small, and rifting and breakup occur relatively quickly, so that the spatiotemporal relationship between rifting and other events is potentially more easily isolated than for larger rifts between the major continents.

Appendix II Keys to Exercises

II.

1. The spatial distribution of melt in the upper mantle largely determines the mantle's ability to transport melt, which creates oceanic crust.

2. The melt content of the upper mantle can be examined by the magnetotelluric (MT) method, using the good conductivity of partially molten rock.

3. During the next 100 years, sea level is likely to rise because of mountain glaciers and ice caps, and two factors—changes in surface mass balance and changes in dynamics—are responsible for the rise.

4. When the same effective pressures lead to dramatically different moving speeds, hysteresis—a retardation—often occurs. Sugiyama & Gudmundsson (2004) found the increase or decrease of Pe affected the relationship between effective pressure and glacier speed; they showed the hysteresis over short time intervals.

5. When heat stress increases, the labor capacity will go down, which may hamper socio-economic development.

6. Climate change is vital to the local development. More and more studies have been investigating how climate change may influence the labor system and how to get used to that influence.

III.

3. A   6. B   12. C   13. D

Chapter 4

I.

1. The implications of the New Mexico CAHe dates will be described in a future contribution and are not discussed further here.

2. Three-dimensional images of individual conodont elements were rendered from two-dimensional attenuation slices using the software Blob3D version 1.4.

3. To assess how crustal contamination may influence magma composition, we also compiled unpublished whole-rock data on basement samples taken in the region around Mocho-Choshuenco.

4. Although the magnitude of cohesion of intact serpentinite is much greater than that of plate boundary fault rocks, the processes of crack growth and coalescence that occur in these experiments are representative of those that occur in situ.

5. In experiments conducted without pore fluids and at ambient temperature, axial and radial strains (*a* and *r*) were measured with foil gages affixed to the surface of the rock and used to calculate volume strain ($v = a + 2r$).

6. Secondly, the studies of Kahmen et al. (2013a, 2013b) focus on open forest or scrubland plants in a highly monsoonal to arid environment, whereas the paleoenvironment of Foulden Maar was neither monsoonal nor arid.

7. The scenario of local ecology driving physiological changes is plausible; however, there are several key factors why this scenario is less likely than the case for changes in pCO_2 and rainfall as drivers of variation in gc/max/, $\delta^{13}C$ and δD.

8. Dissolved deep water ε_{Nd} at these continental margin locations is likely a function of three variables: (1) the magnitude of the Nd flux from sediment pore fluids; (2) the difference between the εNd value of the overlying water and the pore fluid; and (3) the exposure time to this benthic flux of Nd.

9. The only method by which ε_{Nd} values of surface waters have been successfully reconstructed to date is through the analysis of reductively cleaned planktonic foraminifera.

10. GNSS data were processed kinematically using differential carrier phase positioning.

11. The primary base station was also inoperable during October 2014, leading to an increased baseline length and degraded solutions.

12. Understanding the causal relationship between rain-rate and velocity is complicated by the need to cross-correlate and lag the two time series.

II.

1. in	2. of	3. during	4. of
5. by	6. at	7. during	8. to

III.

4. A	5. B	10. C	15. D

IV.

1. We study both melts and crystals by employing ab initio molecular dynamics simulations based on the planar augmented wavefunctions (PAW) flavor. We used the VASP implementation with the Gamma point for sampling the Brillouin zone and generalized-gradient approximation for the exchange correlation in the PBE96 formulation. We used a kinetic energy cutoff of 550 eV for the planewave basis set and of 800 eV for the augmentation charges. Because of the presence of iron, all simulations, at all volumes and temperatures are spin-polarized. This allows for the magnetic spin of the individual Fe atoms to be consistently computed at every single time step. We initiate the local magnetic moments with 1 magneton-Bohr par Fe atom. This is enough to break the symmetry of the magnetic wavefunctions that will converge to their state within a few steps.

2. Phase and orientation maps of reidite-bearing zircon grains were conducted via electron backscatter diffraction (EBSD) mapping using a TESCAN MIRA3 FE-SEM at Curtin University. EBSD and EDS data were collected simultaneously using Oxford Instruments AZtec acquisition system with a Nordlys EBSD detector and XMax 20 mm Silicon Drift Detector. Panchromatic cathodoluminescence (CL) and additional BSE images were collected using the same instrument. Processing of EBSD data was performed using Oxford Instruments Channel 5.12 software.

3. We use two similar metrics calculated within GB polygons to quantify topographic asymmetry. First, we collected up to 10 topographic profiles from each GB polygon, allowing their lengths to vary, while ensuring that they span the distance between opposing ridge lines and are oriented within 45° of north-south (locations of profiles provided in supplemental material). We use these profiles to compute the ratio of the average along-profile slope on north- and south-facing slopes. Second, we calculate the ratio of the average slope of gridded data measured on north- and south-facing aspects, which we refer to as the average slope ratio.

4. Paleocurrents were measured previously at Kekeya, showing sediment provenance from the south, but no such data exist at Sanju until now. We measured the orientation of 251 imbricated pebbles in the conglomerate beds along the Sanju section to obtain the paleo-flow orientation for provenance analysis. Further, we collected samples from eight fluvial sandstones interbedded with conglomerate layers at Sanju, and two medium-grained sandstones at Kekeya to complement our previous DZFT studies. About 50 zircon grains were randomly selected from most samples for U–Pb and fission-track

double dating by Laser-Ablation ICP Mass Spectrometry (LA-ICP-MS), using the analytical parameters and procedures described in Appendix Table S1. For U–Pb ages, we only accept those data with ⩽ 20% discordance. Analyses are reported as $^{206}Pb/^{238}U$ ages for zircon ages ⩽ 1.0 Ga and $^{207}Pb/^{206}Pb$ ages for grains > 1.0 Ga. DZFT age peaks with 95% confidence interval were determined by Radial Plotter. The analytical details are presented in supplements Figs. S1, S2, and S3, and Table S1.

Chapter 5

assess	**assessment**	available	**availability**
coherent	**coherence**	compatible	**compatibility**
coordinate	**coordination**	dominate	**domination**
emerge	**emergence**	evolve	**evolvement**
hypothesize	**hypothesis**	intensify	**intensification**
infect	**infection**	justify	**justification**
modify	**modification**	occupy	**occupation**
occur	**occurrence**	regulate	**regulation**
refine	**refinement**	substitute	**substitution**
subsidize	**subsidization**	transit	**transition**

I.

1. A   2. C   3. B   4. A   5. A   6. B

II.

1. Most of the Earth's surface is characterized by increases in this value, indicating a near global increase in the intensity of the most extreme precipitation events.

2. This age is very close to a minimum seafloor age estimate of 101 ± 1 Ma from DSDP Site 256, located to the north of the Batavia Knoll, but crucially immediately on the western side of the pseudofault extending northward from the Batavia Knoll.

3. As a result, plates that share an interlocking ridge-transform plate boundary show a degree of coupling, and the strength of the coupling will increase with increasing transform length by requiring the breaking of older crust under shear.

4. The primary base station was also inoperable during October 2014, leading to an

Appendix II Keys to Exercises

increased baseline length and degraded solutions.

5. Using the same criteria noted above, ash B3 (93.67 ± 0.12 Ma; red star in Fig. 2a) is selected as the nominal anchor for the Iona astrochronology (RMSE = 0.121; Table 1).

6. The youngest age model for the Iona core comes from the B6 ash (−0.43 Myr, Table 1), while the oldest one comes from the B7 ash (+0.25 Myr, Table 1).

7. Each of the ashes (with the exception of B3) is associated with three numbers, which have the same meaning as in the Libsack core, although the 2σ total uncertainty does not include stratigraphic correlation uncertainty since the dated ash beds come directly from the Iona core.

8. The magnitude of carbon isotope shifts sometimes observed in the Western Interior Basin (WIB) differs from the standard curve of the English Chalk, most likely reflecting local effects and different substrates (e.g., organic matter vs. carbonate).

9. This result is consistent with field observations that document rapid headward growth of low-order channels, instigated by the exposure of readily disaggregated bedrock beneath a more cohesive soil mantle.

10. Leaves from Phase 1 have relatively high SD and SI (SD = 189 ± 43 mm^{-2}, SI = 10.2 ± 1.4), those from Phase 2 have relatively low SD and SI (SD = 140 ± 70 mm^{-2}, SI = 5.1 ± 0.9), and those from Phase 3 show a return to the high SD and SI values of Phase 1 (SD = 243 ± 67 mm^{-2}, SI = 9.9 ± 2.3) (Appendix A, Table A6).

11. At Site 1165, the $^{40}Ar/^{39}Ar$ thermochronological ages of minerals from pebble-sized IRD fall into two main age populations, one from 487 to 571 Ma (average age 530 Ma) and the other from 1075 to 1191 Ma (average age 1125 Ma) (Fig. 5).

12. Based on these studies, we infer that the 450–600 Ma IRD comes from the local Prydz Bay sector and the 1075–1200 Ma IRD from Wilkes Land east of the Denman Glacier, an area that includes the Aurora Subglacial Basin, over 1,000 km distant from Site 1165.

III.

1. Here, we focus on examining the relief evolution of the westernmost Tibetan Plateau by quantifying the exhumation history of this region in the Rutog and Shiquanhe area.

2. The presence of high relief in western Tibet raises the question of the possible influence

of an older, inherited relief on the present topography.

3. However, analysis of detrital zircons contained in the red beds further north in the Domar area performed by researchers indirectly suggests a Jurassic deposition age.

4. This is a follow-up study of a work by Kramers et al. (2013) on a very unusual diamond-rich rock fragment found in the area of southwest Egypt in the southwestern side of the Libyan Desert Glass strewn field.

5. Nevertheless, in each scenario, knowledge of the movement of mid-depth water between 2,000 and 3,000 m, likely Pacific Deep Water (PDW), is necessary.

6. In addition to the Xe–Q composition, an excess of radiogenic ^{129}Xe (from the decay of short-lived radioactive ^{129}I) is observed.

7. Our study does not confirm the presence of exotic noble gases (e.g., G component) that led Kramers et al. (2013) to propose that Hypatia is a remnant of a comet nucleus that impacted the Earth.

8. The absence of graphite-bearing target rock in this area further supports the conclusions that Hypatia must be extraterrestrial.

9. Comparison of any related predictions with the seismic structure of the deep mantle will improve our understanding of the Earth's long-term evolution.

10. Our digital rock physics approach for determining the bulk electrical conductivity of partially molten rocks has the benefit of having fine control on the physics and material properties of the system.

11. In this work we extend the study by Kramers et al. (2013) with isotopic analyses of all five noble gases in several Mg-sized fragments of Hypatia in two different laboratories (CRPG Nancy, France and ETH Zürich, Switzerland) and with a nitrogen isotope investigation performed both at CRPG (Nancy) and IPG-Paris.

12. An attempt to determine the oxygen isotopic composition in Hypatia by the Nancy Cameca 1280 ion probe failed because of the reduced size of oxygen-bearing phases and the presence of contaminants and important amounts of water.

Appendix II Keys to Exercises

Chapter 6

I.

1. induced   2. underestimated   3. causes

4. replace "which" with "where"

II.

1. The continuity of the diatomite is episodically interrupted by turbidites rich in plant material, which probably represent lakeside slumping.

2. We estimate that rain-induced speed-up events are likely to have a positive contribution to displacement of between 2% and 13% per annum.

3. At first glance, these results seem to conflict with our interpretation that fossil leaves in the Foulden Maar sediments record changes in Ca. However, the anthropogenic Ca rise of the recent past does not provide a good analogy to the Foulden Maar record, due to differences in timescale.

4. In any case, because our samples are located ≥ 140 km east of the proposed Angmong fault, and would be in the hanging wall, this fault should not affect their exhumation history.

5. Our findings may have important implications for future numerical studies and the understanding of various geological processes.

6. Such pressure change may cause deglaciation-triggered melt pumping from the mantle, which in turn may replenish the shallow magmatic reservoirs.

7. This could be related to the rheological properties of these levels which can correspond to relatively plastic clays-rich horizons.

8. It is possible that the 2017 discharge measurements do not reflect longer-term conditions.

9. The crystal-rich magma would have encountered a preexisting structural discontinuity, probably compensating for the lack of buoyancy due to the high crystal cargo and triggering a lateral eruption.

10. During the LGM and the deglacial, turbidity currents may have been triggered by

various mechanisms (earthquakes, storms, hyperpycnal discharge, submarine slope failure), which we are unable to resolve.

11. Compared to Site A and H, Site SA features only a single offshore record that may be unrepresentative for the entire region as absolute values of turbidite frequency and thickness strongly depend on site location.

12. This area of the Natal valley is possibly associated with volcanic seamounts which might be related to the EARS extension tectonics

III.

    2. A   7. B   12. C

IV.

    1. C   2. E   3. A   4. B

Chapter 7

I.

    1. effects   2. delete "which" / which are   3. delete "be"   4. is emerging

    5. grants   6. appreciate   7. the manuscript   8. anonymous

II.

    1. E   2. B   3. D   4. A

III.

1. An alternative explanation for the marine turbidite depositional pattern at site H is related to the decreased moisture supply.

2. According to our continental data, temperatures of the lower mid- and low-latitudes were at the present-day level, or even a few degrees below,

3. In both the Middle and Late Miocene time slice, the higher mid- and high-latitudes were considerably warmer than present, independent of prevailing atmospheric pCO_2 conditions.

4. Although less clear-cut than those at the Perth Abyssal Plain microcontinents, changing

Appendix II Keys to Exercises

plate boundary forces have also been proposed to have played a role in calving both the Seychelles and Jan Mayen microcontinents.

5. Our results are influenced by the timing of our experiments early in the melt season: Much more could be learned by repeating these tests during or after the monsoon season when the subsurface hydrology may become more developed after sustained large inputs to the system.

6. Earthquakes with magnitude reaching Mw 6.1 around the Davie Ridge and Mw 5.7 around the Europa–Bassas da India Islands occurred along the fault zone during the last decades.

7. Although we do not have access to the actual samples from these studies, the chemistry, mineralogy, and preparation procedures are nominally the same as our own, suggesting that there is an additional contribution to the bulk conductivity that cannot be accounted for by separately considering the electrical conductivity of olivine and melt.

8. A self-consistent study in which digital rock physics simulations are supplemented by impedance spectroscopy of the same samples, similar to Watson & Roberts (2011), would be immensely valuable to the field.

9. We speculate the existence of a thin, electrochemically distinct layer at the olivine-melt interface that might may account for the apparent discrepancy between the bulk electrical conductivities measured and those we computed using real partial melt geometries.

10. The electrical conductivity of the deformed sample, measured in the shear direction, overlapped the parallel mixing bound (i.e., electrical conduction through parallel pipes), which is consistent with deformation-induced melt segregation.

11. The Miocene Climate Optimum preceded the MMCT and was characterized by oscillating but reduced ice volume and high sea level.

12. Comparison with results obtained by Singh et al. (2012) indicates that dissolved Nd concentrations of seawater samples collected in June 2012 are generally 15%–25% lower than those of samples collected in November 2008.